In the Margins

In the Margins

A Transgender Man's Journey with Scripture

Shannon T. L. Kearns

WILLIAM B. EERDMANS PUBLISHING COMPANY
GRAND RAPIDS, MICHIGAN

Wm. B. Eerdmans Publishing Co.
4035 Park East Court SE, Grand Rapids, Michigan 49546
www.eerdmans.com

© 2022 Shannon T. L. Kearns
All rights reserved
Published 2022
Printed in the United States of America

28 27 26 25 24 23 22   1 2 3 4 5 6 7

ISBN 978-0-8028-7948-6

Library of Congress Cataloging-in-Publication Data

A catalog record for this book is available from the Library of Congress.

Author's note: This book is true to the best of my recollection and experience. Some names have been changed.

Unless otherwise noted, Scripture quotations are from the Common English Bible.

This book is for all of the trans kids and adults.
May it make the world safer for you.
May it give you space to tell your own stories.
May it help you know just how beloved you are.

Contents

Foreword

Whenever I am asked if I feel 100 percent like a woman, I always answer, "Well, if you've talked with one transgender person, you've talked with exactly one transgender person. I cannot tell you how anyone else feels, but I feel 100 percent like a transgender woman. There are things a cisgender woman knows that I will never know."

As a transgender woman, I come from the borderlands, residing in the liminal space between genders. I will not live long enough to lose my White male privilege, having brought it with me when I transitioned. But since the world receives me as a woman, I am beginning to understand just how much the world is tilted in favor of well-educated White males. When I was a man, I started closer to the finish line than anyone else. I did not know that then. I do now.

Because of my unique perspective, I speak all over the world on issues related to gender inequity. My TED Talks have granted me the privilege of hearing from women on all seven continents, thanking me for validating their experience. Life really is harder for women. I am grateful that my view from the borderlands is helpful to others.

As a pastor and theologian, however, I often think about how much my Christian faith has also changed since I transitioned. I keep thinking that one of these days I should write about it. Now, someone has, and I am happy to say it is a very good book. *In the Margins: A Transgender Man's Journey with Scripture* by Shannon T. L. Kearns brings the stories of faith alive in a delightful way.

From Jacob to Rahab to Ezekiel to the transfiguration of Jesus, Shannon brings his unique perspective to the narratives of Scripture that we all thought we understood. Because he takes the Bible far too seriously to take it literally, Shannon has carefully researched and thoughtfully explored these venerable stories, bringing new insight from the liminal space between genders.

I love Shannon's conviction that resurrection is not a moment, but a process. There is a holy unfolding in this book, as Scripture comes to life in a fresh, accurate, and authentic way. In the process Shannon blesses us with the story of his own resurrection.

Toward the end of all my TED Talks, I have said, "The call toward authenticity is sacred, and holy, and for the greater good." *In the Margins* will call you onto that sacred journey, inviting you into the borderlands where the hard work is done. Let Shannon be your guide, as you delve into these words that have been written for the greater good.

REV. DR. PAULA STONE WILLIAMS
founding pastor, Left Hand Church, Longmont, Colorado
author of *As a Woman: What I Learned about Power, Sex, and the Patriarchy After I Transitioned*

Acknowledgments

To my wife, Ashley Hovell: Your encouragement of me means the world. You have shown me what it means to love and be loved. Thank you. To Sarah LeCount: You have seen me through all stages of life and loved me. I can never thank you enough for your steadiness and friendship. To Brian G. Murphy: I love our work together, but more importantly, thank you for your friendship. Thank you for believing in me, challenging me, and dreaming with me. To Adam Rao: Thank you for being the friend of my heart. My family. For showing up for me, for inspiring me, and for all of the nerdy Bible conversations. I love you. To Rev. Kim Wildszewski and Rev. Stephanie Kershner: Thank you for your friendship, support, and love and for getting me through seminary. To my teachers, Rev. Thomas Beers, Rev. Bryan Bucher, Dr. Frank Benyousky, Prof. Mike Yocum, Dr. Hal Taussig, Dr. Gary Dorrien, Dr. Barbara Lundblad, Dr. Patrick Cheng: Thank you for wisdom, for opening my eyes, for pushing me further.

Acknowledgments

To my coconspirators, Dr. Joy Ladin, Dr. Justin Sabia-Tanis, Rev. Cameron Partridge, Rev. Elle Dowd, Kaya Oakes, and Namoli Brennet: Thank you for being faithful and brilliant, for challenging my thinking and encouraging me.

To my cloud of witnesses: Madeleine L'Engle, Fr. Philip Berrigan, Fr. Daniel Berrigan, Rev. Timothy Fauvell, Susan Bowyer, Timothy Daiber Lee, Howard Kearns, Janice Kearns, Victrene Simpson, Florence Kearns, Jennifer Sweeney Moy, and Lisa Kearns.

To copyeditor Rachel Martens and the team at Eerdmans, especially Trevor Thompson, Jennifer Hoffman, and Kristine Nelson: Thank you for your care with this book and for the encouragement and ease of this process. I'm so grateful.

Introduction

M uch of the work that exists in Christian spaces about LGBTQ+ people falls into two camps. The first camp is centered around the question, Can you be LGBTQ+ and Christian? These books are often written for straight and cisgender audiences and include painstaking detail about the various Bible verses cited to condemn sexual behavior (known as clobber verses) and any gender identity that deviates from a straight/cisgender norm. These books include introductory level information about gender and sexual orientation and the differences between them. While these books are important, the conversation is well hashed out already. The arguments from Scripture haven't substantially changed since Virginia Ramey Mollenkott and Letha Dawson Scanzoni wrote *Is the Homosexual My Neighbor?* originally published in 1978! The conversation about transgender issues has been slower to reach prominence, but Justin Sabia-Tanis's book *Trans-Gender: Theology, Ministry, and Communities of Faith* was originally published in 2003. These two books competently and clearly made the argument that it is, indeed, okay to be LGBTQ+ and Christian. These authors argued with a deep knowledge of Scripture and of the

LGBTQ+ community. Yet, people continue to ask the questions and others continue to attempt to answer.

The second camp is academic in nature. The deep, scholarly work of people like Marcella Althaus Reid and Patrick Cheng go way beyond the basics to explore a queer theology that explodes binaries and explores a more expansive view of God. This work is vital, but for those not trained in academia it can be inaccessible at best.

This book aims for a different target, combining stories from my own life with commentary on biblical texts. It's informed by my deep love of Scripture and my background as a seminary-trained priest. I've written in a way accessible to folks not in academia and starting from the point that yes, of course it's okay to be LGBTQ+. More than that, LGBTQ+ people, especially transgender people, have something vital to teach the church and the world if only the world would listen. My personal story is woven into an exploration of Scripture. It's told from the perspective of a white, transgender man who was raised in a white American evangelical church.

One of the primary critiques of queer and trans theology (and really any theology written from the perspective of marginalized people) is that we are "making God in our own image." This critique ignores an uncomfortable fact: all theology comes from a specific context. There is no theology that is generated from a purely objective place; we've been trained to see white, cisgender, male as the norm and categorize everything else as identity politics. This book names a specific and particular context as a place to start when doing theology. It also says there is something to be gained by reading theology from particular people—not just for people who share those particular identities, but for all people.

When I was born the doctors looked at my body and said, "It's a girl!"—a fate that happens every day to children all over the world. When I was born, my mother had recently reconverted to the evangelical faith of her youth. This confluence of the doctor's proclamation and my mother's reconversion set me on a course that just so happened to be headed for a collision.

The course set before me said I would conform to all sorts of roles both in the church and in the world. I would be gentle, humble, quiet in church, devoted, obedient, not a leader. My life was charted from the moment of that doctor's pronouncement of my gender: how I would dress, how I would behave, and how I would live my life. I would dress modestly in feminine clothes, I would go to church regularly, and I would follow Jesus in a prescribed manner. I would believe a certain way and live a certain way. I would get married to a man and have children. I would raise those children to believe in Jesus the way I did, go to church, and live a certain way. This is how it was done; this is how it's always been done. Except I couldn't do that.

I don't know what other transgender stories you might have read or heard. I don't know what transgender story you might carry in your own flesh and bone. This is my transgender story. A story that is bound together with theology and church and Scripture. I cannot help but speak in scriptural metaphor because that was the language with which I was raised. When I was born, I was wrapped in pink blankets and swaddled with evangelical theology. The blankets, like the theology, would one day threaten to suffocate me. I needed to be unbound, just like Lazarus when he came out of the tomb (see John 11:44).

This is the story of my unbinding. But it's also the story of how you, too, can be unbound. Unbound from beliefs that have grown too tight and threaten to choke the life out of you. Unbound from outdated notions of gender and gender roles. Unbound from only reading Scripture in one way, through one lens. Unbound from all that no longer gives you, me, and us life.

3

In this book you'll find my story, Scripture's stories, and hopefully at least a window into your own story. I believe in stories—in the power they have to heal, transform, and reimagine ourselves and the world. It's not a coincidence that the record we have of our Christian faith is a collection of stories. Stories that argue with one another, stories that contradict each other, stories that are messy and confusing and complicated. These stories are written by people, just like you and me, struggling to make sense of the world and their place in it. Struggling to make sense of their relationship with the Creator, the source of life who also manages to remain a mystery.

Even though I grew up reading Scripture, having it read to me, memorizing portions of it as a Bible quizzer, and believing it had the power to transform my life, I missed a lot. Had I really read it, I would have seen stories of gender nonconformity, of people going outside of the bounds of what they were told their life needed to look like, of questions and arguments even with God about identity. I read Scripture but I was locked into a way of interpreting it that left no room for exploration. I was told how to read it and what it meant. It wasn't until I was an adult and able to read with fresh eyes that I unearthed all of the goodness that Scripture had to offer and all of the ways it spoke, even to me as a transgender person. Reading with new eyes and delving into the text again changed my life. It changed how I tell my own story.

When we tell our stories we invite others to listen, to connect, and to hopefully feel less alone. We beckon others to see the world, even briefly, through someone else's eyes. To practice empathy. My story is just my own; I cannot speak for all transgender people everywhere. I do believe, however, that transgender people have unique insights into life and faith that can enrich people who don't have our experience of the world. We know what it is to not fit in, to have to fight for a place for ourselves in the world and in the church. We know what it is to look for ourselves in stories and to mostly feel invisible. We know what it is to write our own stories. And because we know these things, we are able to teach others how to look, how to see, how to write.

Whether you are transgender or cisgender, whether you are an evangelical or an exvangelical, whether you were raised with Scripture or are just dipping your toes in for the first time, I pray there is something here that is a balm for your soul. I hope you find comfort for your journey. I hope you feel less alone.

Eunuchs: Beyond Boundaries

I n elementary school, my best friend was Chris, the boy who lived across the street from me. We were the same age, and in the summers we would play outside from sunup to sundown. We rode bikes and went swimming; we spied on the neighbors and trekked through the woods. There were days of epic mud fights and endless baseball games with a dizzying array of complexity and "ghost" runners since there were only two of us.

We created worlds and inhabited them—mysteries involving rocks we found in the stream, a day-long fantasy where we played imagined characters, and conspiracy theories about neighbors who we thought never left their houses. As a child, I had no deep understanding of gender; I was simply myself. I loved my dolls and my stuffed animals, but I also loved my Teenage Mutant Ninja Turtles and my Micro Machines. I collected baseball cards and loved puffy stickers. I wore dresses to church on Sundays and then came home and put on my shorts and t-shirts and ran around in the yard and woods. There seemed to be no disconnect between myself and the world.

I felt at one with myself and everything around me. I would go hunting with my grandfather and then play parent and teacher with my dolls. I would play with Chris outside all day and then come home and read Babysitters Club books until it was time to fall asleep. I didn't have a sense that anything I was doing was gendered.

There were occasional moments where gender would confine me: wanting to cut my hair short and not being allowed; quitting T-ball and then not signing up for a team for years because I wanted to play real baseball, not softball; continually asking if I could wear pants to church "just this once" and being told to put on a skirt. Sometimes, adults would ask me questions about my appearance, such as, "Why do you wear that baseball cap all the time?" When I would reply, "I just like it," they'd respond knowingly, "Oh, you'll grow out of it." I would laugh and then run outside to play again.

I've never been a morning person. My most active mental times, even as a kid, happened late in the evening. It took forever to get my brain to settle down enough for me to sleep. And yet I had a strict 8:30 p.m. bedtime. I would get into bed and my mind would race and I would stare at the ceiling begging for sleep. Early on, I learned to tell myself stories to help pass the time until I could drift off.

I imagined myself as a professional baseball player making the World Series–winning triple play. I imagined myself as a soldier on the battlefield in the army saving everyone in my platoon. I was always the hero; I was also, almost always, a boy. Sometimes in my stories, I would tell myself that I was born a boy; in others, I had somehow turned into a boy. These stories were a way of making space for myself to inhabit a world I felt I belonged in. I never told anyone about my stories. These stories were so vivid they sometimes felt more real than the life I was living. I would drift into them on the bus on my way to a school where I often felt out of place. I had friends, but I was always kind of on the outskirts. The elementary school I went to was affiliated with a strict independent Baptist church. Their rules made my evangelical church look like an anything goes free for all. The Baptists had rules about everything: from hemlines and the importance of boys wearing belts, to outlawing denim and prohibiting the use of drums in worship. This is a school that, well into the 1990s, was still administering corporal punishment to their students.

Even though I was a devout Christian who went to church, I didn't go to the church affiliated with the school. I felt their rules were a little over the top. I wore shorts under the mandatory skirts so I could play better during recess, and when I was alone on the bus on the way home, the last to be dropped off, I would take off my skirt and enjoy the freedom of just being in my shorts. I felt out of step with my classmates, so I retreated into books and my imagination. I realized the world of stories gave me the escape I was longing for. I gave myself what my mom called a "play name." It was a masculine name I used when I envisioned myself as a baseball player or army guy. I used it as a pen name when I wrote stories. I didn't know at the time it was also my father's first name (he died when I was very young and I never knew him), but I claimed Timothy as my play name. Years later, when I transitioned, I took it as one of my middle names, a way of honoring both my dad and the boyhood I had tried to carve for myself.

When I was a child, our church put on annual musicals for the congregation. Every year I was excited to audition and find out what role I would get. One time, we did a musical called *All We Like Sheep* where we played—you guessed it—sheep who spent a lot of time talking about how good our shepherd was. It was a little on the nose, but cute kids in sheep costumes are always a hit with adults.

The year I remember most fondly was the one when we performed a Psalty musical. For those readers who didn't grow up immersed in the very strange pop culture world of 1990s American evangelicalism, Psalty was a cartoon character in a series of children's programming. He was a giant blue hymnal (i.e., psalter) that walked and talked. He had a hymnal family. An adult from our congregation and his daughter created and dressed in these elaborate, giant hymnbook costumes.

There was a series of musicals written for churches that featured Psalty, and the one we were doing that particular year was *Psalty the Singing Songbook's Hymnological Adventure through Time*. In this musical, the giant blue songbook took a group of kids time traveling to different ages where hymns were being written. The musical covered everything from the temple songs of the Levitical priests, to the future King David as a child turning poetry into music, to Fanny Crosby writing in the 1850s.

I was chosen to play King David, a male character. I was thrilled. I got to sing a solo in Hebrew and lead a dance circle. Plus, I got to pretend to be a boy! I loved every second of it. I wore my long hair in a tight braid with a headband covering it. I was dressed in a white tunic and I felt so cool. While some people teased me about playing a boy, I let that roll off my shoulders because I was so happy. I was doing what I loved in a role that felt like *me*. It was the sense of ease I had in this role that I didn't have in my "real life" that made it feel so special.

Things started to shift when I turned twelve. I was less and less comfortable in the skirts I had to wear for my conservative Christian school and church on Sundays. I would wear shorts underneath "for playing on the jungle gym," but really it was because shorts felt more comfortable. I didn't know what to do with my growing body, and getting my period terrified me. I was embarrassed to talk about bodily things. I wanted to disappear.

Our church celebrated communion quarterly. We did it so infrequently because it was a huge production that took most of the evening. We would all come to church and gather together for prayer and singing. Then it was time for the part I hated most, the foot washing. The women would go to one room and the men would go to another. I always felt out of place during this sorting, though I couldn't have told you why at the time. Everyone would take off their socks and shoes and bowls of water would be passed from one person to the next. When the bowl came to you, you put your feet in it, and the person next to you got down on their knees and washed your feet and dried them with the towel wrapped around their waist. Then you would both stand and embrace, the towel would be passed to you, and you would get on your knees and wash the feet of the person next to you. During this entire process hymns would be sung from memory.

I was terrified of the foot washing. I was always glad it came first before communion so we could get it out of the way. Even as we drove to church my stomach would be in knots. I didn't want to do the foot washing. I would often try to get out of it, but everyone participated. I didn't like being barefoot. I didn't like people touching my feet. I didn't like touching someone else's feet. This wasn't some kind of weird foot phobia; it was the intimacy that scared me. This sense of being seen by other people, being touched and held—I didn't want it. I tried to make sure I only washed my mother's feet, which seemed easier somehow. She would roll her eyes as I tried to position myself to the correct side of her so I would wash her feet.

Once the foot washing was complete, we would sit around long tables and share a full meal, family style. I generally found the meals to be fine, but we weren't supposed to have casual conversation. We were supposed to talk about what it would be like when we were all in heaven together, to think about eternity, and to talk about our spiritual lives. I mostly just wanted to eat and talk about how the Phillies were doing, so those meals got pretty boring. I always left feeling a little hungry, though, like there was never enough food. My mom would remind me this was a spiritual symbol: we weren't supposed to be gorging ourselves on food. The explanation didn't make my stomach feel any better.

After dinner we would listen to a sermon and Scripture reading about the importance of the bread and the cup. We would be reminded to make ourselves right with God, because if we took part in communion with sin in our lives, we would die. As a kid with an active imagination and a pretty firm idea that God was ready to smite me at any given moment, the quiet time of prayer before we took communion consisted of me praying frantically that God would forgive me for whatever I'd done wrong, even the things I didn't know were wrong, or the wrong things I didn't remember doing. We were given time to go and apologize to people in the congregation we might have wronged. I kept wondering if someone was waiting for me to apologize to them or if I had slighted someone without even realizing it. I took the bread and the cup and waited for lightning to strike, sure that I had somehow prayed incorrectly or been living in sin.

When I recount the stories in an orderly progression like this, it seems clear I was grappling with my gender identity from a young age. I can point to all of the places where I violated gender norms and where my behavior didn't fit the roles set out for me. Someone trying to make a case against transgender identity could do the same thing with this same set of stories and point to how I played with dolls, how I never said I was a boy out loud, and how I didn't mind wearing dresses when I was small. The arguments over when I knew and if I was born transgender don't appeal to me, though; neither do arguments about nature versus nurture. What I do find interesting is how I dealt with growing up in strictly gendered spaces without the language of gender.

I had no idea transgender people even existed. Since I didn't have that word in my vocabulary, I don't remember ever thinking that I might be transgender. I was definitely confused, because I knew something about my body felt off to me. Some days I felt like I was trying to come out of my own skin, that it was holding me in a shape that didn't match my soul, but I had no language about gender or gender variance. My world was rigidly divided into male and female. Men did "manly" things like lead and preach and build stuff. Women did "womanly" things like dress modestly and care for children and work in the church kitchen. The two spheres were mostly separate except for the strange land that was marriage.

Men went off for their men's weekends, hunting and doing whatever else men did when they got together. Women stayed home or threw showers for weddings and babies. I didn't get to go on the hunting weekends. I hated the showers because they were unbearably boring to me. Plus, I felt nervous around all of these women who seemed to understand with such clarity how to move through the world in their bodies. They seemed comfortable talking about marriage and babies. They were happy to be surrounded by pink things. Each woman talked about her husband- or baby-to-be with shyness, but also with a deep joy.

Years later I realized that some (most?) of my discomfort came from these strictly gendered spaces. Even before I had words to express myself, I had the sense I wasn't sure I belonged in these spaces. Being in a space where I didn't belong yet was also required to be vulnerable felt wrong somehow.

My sense of gender growing up is conflicted; on the one hand, outside and at play either alone or with my friend Chris, I had a sense of myself as ungendered and free. At church and school I felt out of step but didn't know why. Had you asked me then I wouldn't have pointed to gender as the root of my unease, but looking back, it's clearly the culprit.

What I do know is growing up without language about gender was difficult. I didn't know how to express what I was feeling, so I simply didn't. I felt both a sense of fearlessness in being myself and also carried shame about feeling like I was failing to measure up. I didn't understand the shame, though. I just knew I wasn't like the other girls.

As I grew older my gender difference became more pronounced. I started to get more grief for being different, but it was almost always subtle. No one, at least in the beginning, directly asked me about my sexuality or gender presentation. There were simply gentle nudges: I was told I should wear a dress, asked if I wanted to grow my hair longer, queried about whether there were any boys I was interested in. No one said I was failing at being a girl, but I was taught the Bible was clear on everything, particularly how men and women were supposed to live in the world. I knew I was not meeting the expectations that were "clearly" laid out in Scripture. It turns out, though, like much of what I was taught about the Bible growing up, that isn't true. There is a whole world of gender complexity and expansiveness in our Scriptures. You just have to know where to look! Had I known then what I know now about gender and Scripture, I would have had a much different experience growing up.

In Sunday school and church services during my childhood, I never noticed how often eunuchs are talked about throughout Scripture, which is probably because I didn't know to look for them or understand how transgressive and radical they were.

When the Israelites were forced into exile by the Babylonians, some of their men were taken and forcibly castrated (2 Kings 20:18).[1] These castrated people were called eunuchs, and many eunuchs were placed to serve in the courts of their captors. Their castration meant they wouldn't be a threat to the paternity lines of the elite.

Eunuchs were considered to be ungendered; they were no longer men, but they weren't women either. They were their own class of gender. While it's impossible to make a direct correlation to transgender and nonbinary people of today due to their forced castration, eunuchs are one of the closest comparisons we have. When we look at how people understood and treated eunuchs in the past, the parallels with transgender and nonbinary people are hard to ignore. Eunuchs weren't treated as castrated men; they were treated as a whole new gender. Not men, but also not women. In between. They moved through royal palaces freely, slipping between the men's areas and the women's areas.

Even though these eunuchs were in places of power and living more comfortable lives than the hard laborers, those places of power must have been cold comfort. They were now cut off from having biological children. Maybe in the time of exile they didn't much care, because survival was top of mind. They were alive; they would deal with the implications of castration later. When Israel was sent into exile, the people had to figure out the answers to several questions. What decisions would they make in order to save their lives? What kind of compromises would God forgive? How would they keep their faith alive when they no longer had the temple to worship in and when those in the priestly class were scattered or killed?

When exile ended, the Israelites had to deal with the fallout. The texts that we have in our Bibles today mostly come from the post-exilic period when the newly reunited community was trying to figure out how to recover from decisions made in exile. There were different ideas about how to create a community again, and we have these arguments from within the community recorded in Scripture. In the book of Deuteronomy, the focus is on purity (see especially Deut. 22–23). The idea was that exile had been caused by a community filled with impurities. The Israelites had become too much like the nations around them and if they were to survive, if they were to become a thriving nation again, they would need to regain their sense of communal purity. So, rules about who was "in" and who was "out" were created. Rules were established about who could worship and who couldn't.[2]

The creation of a class of ungendered or third gender people in exile was a complication for the people of Israel. From the very beginning of the Israelite people, the focus had been on procreation and family. For a small and often oppressed nation, numbers mattered. Having children meant that you were increasing the population, but it also meant that you would have people to care for you in your old age. Children were everything. Eunuchs, those whose testicles had been crushed, were now prevented access to the temple (see Deut. 23:1–3).

The eunuchs were being sent home from exile, but they were no longer able to be a part of the community in the same way. What a blow. Insult added to injury. Where did eunuchs belong in this new Israel? Where could they belong? These questions were about more than just religious observance; they were now also having to face the reality that there would be no families or offspring for them. No children to care for them in their old age. They were released from captivity, yes, but at what cost? Where were they supposed to go? What were they supposed to do? Who were they now? Their undoing was complete.

Yet Deuteronomy doesn't contain the whole story. There are other texts, written at the same time, that argue with Deuteronomy. We need to understand the Bible as a library, a collection of books in conversation with one another. While there are through lines in Scripture, there are also internal arguments and contradictions. These texts represent a people grappling to make sense of their place in the world, their relationship with the Divine, and why things were happening the way they were happening. Thankfully, we have these arguments recorded! We aren't left with just the prohibition of eunuchs and foreigners in Deuteronomy (Deut. 23:1), we're also provided with the counterpoints: the story of Ruth saying that foreigners should be welcomed arguing with the text of Ezra saying foreigners should be banished or killed (Ezra 10:10–11 and following). The laws of Deuteronomy (Deut. 23:1) prohibiting access to temple worship by eunuchs while Isaiah (Isa. 56:3–5) says they'll be given a name better than sons and daughters. The book of Esther making the case for eunuchs being the reason the Israelites survived at all, thus elevating eunuchs' status significantly.[3] We need to read Scripture as a conversation, and the conversation about eunuchs is provocative.

In Isaiah 56:3b–5, we read a rebuttal to Deuteronomy. The prophet says, "And don't let the eunuch say, 'I'm just a dry tree.' The Lord says: To the eunuchs who keep my sabbaths, choose what I desire, and remain loyal to my covenant. In my temple and courts, I will give them a monument and a name better than sons and daughters. I will give to them an enduring name that won't be removed."

It's a word of comfort and hope. A word of healing. It's an assurance their survival will not be their undoing. Eunuchs are told they will be given an enduring legacy. This piece about being given an "enduring name" rings loudly for many transgender and nonbinary people, especially the ones who have claimed new names or who might be unable to birth or conceive children. This also rings loudly for the many people who have felt excluded and cut off from entry into religious spaces because of their gender diversity.

Eunuchs show up all throughout Scripture at often pivotal moments. They are able to move between worlds and as such can be

messengers, like in Esther, leading to rescue. Even though they often show up in moments of crisis, leading up to salvation, I wonder
if they, like me, felt that razor-wire tension of fear and comfort.
Gladness that their lives had been spared, but a question about the
cost of that salvation. Did they feel continually out of place? As they
moved between worlds, as they were considered ungendered, did
they feel in their very bodies their unbelonging? Where were they
supposed to fit? Where were they supposed to make their home?
Did they feel their bodies were betraying them? Did they feel like
they weren't at home in any gendered space? Did they only feel
comfortable with the other eunuchs?

Writing about eunuchs is complicated because their experiences come from a very different time and place. It's dangerous
to try to read twenty-first-century identities back onto ancient
people, especially when the eunuchs' identities were often a result
of trauma. The idea of nature versus nurture didn't yet exist, nor
did ideas about claiming individual identity. We don't know how
eunuchs would identify today. Would they claim to be part of the
intersex community? Would they claim their maleness? Would
they desire to be under the transgender umbrella? We just don't
know. There's also the issue of consent: most of the eunuchs we
encounter in Scripture were castrated against their will. They were
victims harmed during warfare. They were people dominated by
oppressive systems.

In some ways, it's vital not to compare forced castration to the
lives and identities of transgender people today—trans people who
know who they are, who have to fight to claim their identity, who
have to jump through Kafkaesque hoops in order to be able to live
as their true selves. And yet, even in Scripture, we have a hint of
choice about gender. When Jesus teaches about eunuchs in Matthew 19:12, he talks about those who have "made themselves eu-

nuchs." The entire verse reads: "For there are eunuchs who have been eunuchs from birth. And there are eunuchs who have been made eunuchs by other people. And there are eunuchs who have made themselves eunuchs because of the kingdom of heaven. Those who can accept it should accept it."

We don't entirely know what he means by this; commentators and theologians have argued about this verse for decades. Given how often translations are marked as "unclear" when a translator doesn't want to deal with the implications, and with how often passages are straightwashed (the practice of assuming everyone is heterosexual and reading all things through that lens), we are left uncertain about the context and meaning of this verse. But Jesus certainly seems to be saying that there were at least some people who castrated themselves in the name of the kingdom. There were some people who lived outside of the boundaries of gender in order to fulfill what they saw as their duty to God.

My experience with transition was that I couldn't really be close to God until I could make peace with my body. Until I could move through the world as I knew I was intended to. My transition was a homecoming, a process of making peace, a fulfillment of my calling. When Jesus said he came so we would have abundant life (John 10:10), I think this is part of what he's talking about: being who we are, all of who we are. Living our fullest and truest lives, which means being honest (if only with ourselves) about who we are meant to be.

While we can't know exactly how eunuchs identified, we do know that they are the closest comparison we have to modern-day trans-gender and nonbinary people. We can see correlations in the ways they were treated, how they were considered a part (or not a part) of their community, and how they moved through the world.

One of the most well-known eunuchs is the eunuch from Ethiopia in Acts 8. (While today there are a number of gender-neutral pronouns, we don't know what pronouns this person might have used, so I will use the singular "they" to refer to them.) We don't know their name, only that they are a high-powered official in the court of the queen. They are a God-worshipper, interested in the God of the temple in Jerusalem. They are learned and wealthy, they have access and ability, and yet when we meet them they are on a wilderness road, traveling home from Jerusalem after attempting to worship at the temple. I say attempting because in light of Jewish law, they wouldn't have been allowed to even enter the temple, let alone worship.

We often talk about this story as one of a person's conversion to Christianity, about someone who is so captivated by the Jesus story they immediately want to be baptized. The story is representative of a conversion experience, but it's also about someone who desperately wants to worship and is turned away. It's about someone who is an "Other" on many fronts: not Jewish (that we know of), a foreigner, from the "ends of the earth" (Acts 1:8) and, of course, a sexual and gender outsider.

Yet Philip doesn't tell the eunuch they aren't allowed because of their gender. Philip doesn't tell the eunuch they need to behave differently. They simply believe in Jesus and are baptized. By claiming baptism, the eunuch throws open the doors of faith in Jesus to new people. They reimagine for everyone what this new Jesus movement could be and do. It's a rewriting of the boundaries of who is in and who is out. It's a radical reordering of the rules.

ᏅᏅ

The examples of eunuchs throughout Scripture resonate for modern readers in several ways. First, they are records of empathy for people who feel forced into places they don't belong. These feelings track with those of transgender men trying to navigate the world of women, the transgender women trying to survive in masculine spaces. These are people who know where they belong but sometimes struggle to find a way into that space, both before and after transition. They feel forced, for a time at least, into a space they don't belong in and don't really know how to navigate. They can sense there is something off but maybe can't even articulate what it is.

There are also the people for whom the binaries don't fit. Who struggle to feel at home anywhere, not because of something inside of them, but because the structure of the world is set up to prioritize binaries above everything else. Nonbinary people who live outside of binary gender give us a window into how hard it is to exist in that space. They grapple with everything from clothing to gender drop-down menus, to restrooms, to language that doesn't fit. When they declare their truth, they are met with pushback and a lack of understanding. They are told their pronouns aren't "grammatically correct" or they are "too hard to remember" or they are "just weird." Their very presence is met with a lack of respect for their wonderfully unique humanity.

What does it cost us to honor another person's experience and identity? What does it cost us to use the name and pronouns that are correct? What does it cost us to offer empathy even if we lack understanding? It doesn't cost much—maybe a bit of discomfort, maybe stumbling on a learning curve, maybe some relational mistakes that feel embarrassing.

On the flip side, what does our lack of honoring others cost? Our refusal to use correct names and pronouns? Our refusal to offer empathy? The cost is deadly, but cisgender people are not the ones to pay it. The burden is on those who are already oppressed and marginalized; the cost is paid by the very people who cannot afford to pay it.

Another lesson we can learn from the examples of eunuchs in Scripture is that their witness can give us a glimpse into the pain of living in this Othered space, both the spaces where we struggle to fit in and the spaces that were never designed for us in the first place. So much of the pressure transgender and nonbinary people face is from the expectations other people place on us. Expectations about what it means to be a woman or a man. Expectations about how to move through the world in a body that is coded as a certain sex. Expectations that every person will fit into one of two boxes. When we don't live up to these expectations, when we cross binaries and boundaries, or when we live outside of the binaries and boundaries all together, we are often punished. People try to push us back into the boxes so we don't upset the status quo. We are told that we need to be recognizable to cisgender people, that we need to conform so as not to make other people confused or uncomfortable.

When the first question asked of a pregnant person is "Do you know what you're having?" and the expected answer is an either/or response of "boy" or "girl," we have a problem. We begin to categorize people even before they are born, fitting them into boxes and along with those boxes a whole host of expectations. Expectations that are fueled and informed by the binary world we live in and that have nothing to do with this new person just about to enter the world.

One of the most hurtful things a transgender person can hear after they come out is, "I feel like my [child, spouse, friend, and so on] died. I am grieving." It's hurtful on multiple levels. Often the transgender person who has come out is feeling alive for the first time in their life. They are feeling connected to their body and identity in a new way. They have chosen to be honest about that with the people closest to them and the people closest to them react as if they are dead when they are standing right in front of them.

The cisgender person who is grieving will retort that they are grieving what they had envisioned for their life and the life of their child/spouse/friend. But those visions may not be rooted in genuine connection or understanding of the person upon whom those expectations are placed. The cisgender parents might vocally grieve the grandchildren they won't have without ever asking if their child planned to have children. Or, if they might have another plan for having children (like surrogacy or adoption). The cisgender mother might grieve the discarded future wedding dress or the mother/son dance without ever asking or considering that her child may have never wanted those things in the first place. The transgender person may feel doubly blamed for failing to live up to gendered expectations. They may unfairly be blamed for a grief of which they are not the cause.

Certainly a cisgender person whose loved one comes out might feel a mix of emotions, but when they express those emotions as grief to a transgender person, they are doing harm. When you tell a transgender person that you feel like they've died when they are, in fact, standing right in front of you alive and well, you are saying that your expectations and desires for their life are more important than their own expectations and desires. You are telling them your feelings and expectations are more important than their lived reality, your comfort is more important than theirs, your dreams for their life are more important than their own dreams.

Instead of expressing blame, you can welcome this new information. Be glad they trusted you enough to reveal the truth about themselves. Honor their revelation with grace and compassion. Work out your hard feelings with a therapist and root out your own discomfort. Coming out is a vulnerable time, and you can make it less fraught by preparing to come to terms with areas of internalized transphobia or gendered expectations and meeting your loved one with unconditional love and support.

We live in a hyper-gendered society, and not just within the evangelical Christian subculture. Take a stroll through the baby clothes section of any store and see what you find. Blue onesies labeled "for boys" that say "I'm here for the boobies." Pink frills on outfits labeled "for girls" that say "I'm Daddy's princess." Before our children can even speak, we are putting them into gendered boxes. Boxes that come not only with colors, but with an entire lifetime of gendered expectations. Expectations that say these children will not only grow up identifying with the gender they were assigned at birth but that they will also be heterosexual and desire marriage. If we look even deeper, these clothes could be understood as a prediction of how our children will develop harmful ideas about what it means to be a man or a woman.

Someone might argue that less than 1 percent of the US population is transgender, so what does it matter if we promote gender "norms" for the majority? Odds are these kids dressed in blue or pink onesies will grow up to identify with the gender they were assigned at birth. And since only 5 percent or so of the entire US population is LGB, odds are in the heterosexuals' favor.[4] Any time we place restrictions on our children before they can even speak to us, we are shaping the way they move through their world. If your child looks at their baby photos and sees picture after picture of blue outfits and toy trucks and guns, will they really feel comfortable telling you that's not how they identify? What if they are a boy, but want to play with dolls instead? Will there be space for them to express their gender differently?

When we talk about gender, people often think we're talking only about queer and trans folks, or women's issues. They don't see the larger picture of how all of us are caught up in a system of gender that is literally killing us. From men who refuse to see doctors because they are "tougher" than their medical issue, to doctors who refuse to believe women when they say they are in pain, to trans folks who struggle to receive any health care at all, this system of rigid boxes and binaries impacts our physical health on a daily basis.[5]

Gender also impacts our mental health. Men are told not to feel things and definitely not to talk about the things they feel. They are expected to be strong and silent and stoic. When they can't, they are shamed and pushed back into their boxes. Women are expected to shoulder all of the household tasks, raise the children, and often work a full-time job on top of that. The emotional labor of managing the household goes unrewarded, unpaid, and takes a toll. The mental health toll of living in this kind of gendered society for trans and gender nonconforming people is fraught. Suicide rates of trans kids are astronomically higher than their cisgender peers, not because being trans makes you depressed, but because living in a world that isn't built for you takes a significant toll.[6]

What would happen if we simply allowed people to be and live without gendering items, spaces, and activities? If we started to break down the boxes of "this is what men do" and "this is what women do" and instead allowed people to find where they fit? Relaxing and then eliminating these boxes would create space for people to be able to move and breathe. Like the eunuchs in the Bible who moved between men's and women's spaces, we'd have freedom to experiment and try and find our own balance.

The alternative is prolonging the pain we feel of not living up to someone else's expectations, of not fitting in anywhere, of feeling like a failure for simply being ourselves. We should want better for our children. We should want better for ourselves.

Imagine a world where the goal was healthy and whole human beings. Where the goal was emotional health and intelligence. Where the goal wasn't to fit in or be a certain way but it was simply to be whole. Doesn't that sound lovely?

Beyond gender and sexuality, there are all sorts of boxes we find ourselves in. Boxes of belief and behavior. Boxes of expectations and desire. Think of all of the ways your life has been shaped by someone else. The pressure to get the right grades in school and take certain classes, the drive to go to a good college so you can get a good job, the redirection from humanities and the arts and toward math and science, the push toward a certain type of relationship. We all find ourselves bumping up against what other people expect of us. Sometimes we acquiesce because it's easier than fighting the system and it doesn't cost us very much, but sometimes those compromises eat away at our souls and cause us damage.

I think of the young man in one of my youth groups who said he would do nice things for other people after he retired, but he had to make a lot of money first. He was fifteen, and already he was being indoctrinated into a certain way of viewing the world. He was developing a view that would dictate everything he did, from his schooling to his choice of jobs, to how he spent and saved his money. His life was already laid out for him and it didn't include things like service to others. I tried my best to offer an alternative viewpoint, but the weight of familial and societal expectations was too strong for my voice to break through in one hour each Sunday morning.

How many of us are trapped by similar ideas? How many of us put our calling on the back burner until after the debt is paid off or the kids are through college or the grandkids are in school? How many of us tell ourselves that we'll be who we're meant to be later— we just have to get through this stage of life first?

How many of us stay in places that no longer welcome us because we feel like we have to? We have to stay in the church that doesn't let LGBTQ+ people serve because all of our friends are there, and we have to save them. We stay in a theological system that no longer meets our spiritual needs because if we don't, God will send us to hell. We stay in a marriage that is deeply unhealthy because we don't want to face the shame of divorce.

We stay in our boxes because they feel safer. We're told that if we leave them, we'll be thrown out, cast away. But we were never meant to live in boxes.

The message of the eunuchs is that the boxes don't work. They aren't fit to live in. They will likely kill us if we stay there. The freedom to move between spaces and worlds, the freedom to claim all of who we are, the freedom to be is what we are called to. The message of the eunuchs also calls us to look around and ask: Who is being excluded? Who is not welcome? Who is there no space for? That list of people and those names that come to your mind? The message in Isaiah 56 and from the story of the Ethiopian eunuch in Acts 8 says, "There is space for them in the kingdom of God, too." There is nothing to prevent them from being baptized. There is nothing to prevent them from worshipping. They don't need to change to be worthy; they are made worthy by wanting to be included.

Anyone who desires the water is welcome.

Joseph: The Dreamer

'm sitting cross-legged on top of a picnic table underneath a canopy. Around me, my teammates yell and laugh and splash one another as they jump into the pool. I am fully clothed in baggy shorts and an extra-large t-shirt. My ever-present baseball cap sits on my head. If anyone asks, I tell them I'm not swimming because of my solidarity with the girls on the team who are on their periods and can't swim today, but the reality is the thought of the locker room after an already stressful day just doesn't feel like fun. I'd rather sit out from the swimming instead of dealing with the panic public locker rooms instill in me.

I sit and I watch the activity around me. I'm nervous because I am surrounded by the female adult leaders on my team. They want to talk to me. Shelly starts, as she usually does.

"A couple of people at the last church mentioned to us they think it's strange you only wear one earring."

I shrug. "I just like wearing the one. I did research it. I'm wearing it in the ear that means you're not gay."

I laugh; they do not. I'm not savvy enough to realize this is the exact wrong thing to say.

Debbie tries to appease me, "Would you be willing to put in the other earring?"

"It doesn't mean much to me. I'll just take it out!"

I reach up and remove the earring and tuck it into the pockets in my cargo shorts. The leaders frown.

It would take me years to realize in this moment I think I am being easy going and cooperative, but the leaders see that I would rather not do something I want to do than put the second earring in. For them this is an act of defiance against femininity. It's yet another way I am failing to live up to expectations that make no sense to me. I'm walking through a minefield I don't even realize is armed. Defenseless.

I'm spending my summer on Operation Barnabas. It's an eight-week mission trip for junior and senior high school students in the Grace Brethren Church. We're traveling from church to church in a sky-blue painted school bus without air conditioning. At each church, we do a variety of "encouragement ministries" because Barnabas, helper to the apostle Paul in the Bible, was known as the Son of Encouragement. Our duties vary from church to church, but it's usually some combination of running Vacation Bible Schools, handing out fliers door to door for church events, doing programs (never performances) for Sunday morning services, and the one constant: manual labor.

We sleep in church fellowship halls and basements on the floor. We eat whatever the church decides to provide us. Occasionally we get to stay in host homes and sleep in a real bed, but those nights feel rare. We are never alone. We're supposed to get an hour each day to have time to read our Bibles and pray but up to this point on the trip we've yet to get that hour. As an introvert I am crumbling under the pressure. The extroverts on the team are in their glory, feeding off of the constant motion and energy. I wonder, not for the first time, how in the world I ended up here.

I never intended to apply for this mission trip, even though it was expected of me. Operation Barnabas (called OB for short. Yes. Really.) was considered the culmination of a Grace Brethren student's high school experience. The best Christians went on OB. The students who were leaders. The ones who were expected to do great things for God. In my home church I was considered part of that crew. I was well liked by my youth group leaders. I was devout and dedicated to my faith. I had been on mission trips before. I was a leader in my youth group. I had started all sorts of ministries; a drama team, a mime team, a contemporary youth ensemble. I was part of small groups and Bible studies. I was at the church so often they gave me my own set of keys so church staff wouldn't have to keep coming to let me into the building. I was trusted.

And yet I had no interest in Operation Barnabas for one very specific reason: the showers.

I had heard stories about the showers on OB, how teams were often traveling and using YMCA or high school locker rooms in order to get their daily shower in. There was no privacy in these showers, everyone just got naked and showered out in the open. If you had asked me directly, I would have said I was just really modest, but deep down, down in a part of me that I barely had any words for, I was filled with dread about the idea of being seen. And the idea of seeing. Or, more specifically, I feared that if people really saw me, they would think I was looking at their bodies. I could do without that kind of stress in my life, especially right before I went off to college and right after a year when my mother and stepfather went through a messy divorce. Why would I go out of my way to suffer for an entire summer? No, thank you. I'd stay home and work and save up some money.

But then Operation Barnabas came to our church. Participants seemed older, even the teens I knew well from my youth group seemed different, transformed by their time on this trip. I watched them as they hung out together, having bonds that I couldn't even imagine. I watched as they led worship services and shared their testimonies. At the end of the service when they asked who was going to answer the call to join the trip next year, I found myself standing up. I didn't know why. I didn't want to be standing up. I desperately did NOT want to go on this trip. Yet my body stood up and my feet walked down the aisle after the service to get my application.

In the car on the way home I blurted out, "I don't know why . . . don't ask me, but I feel like I have to apply to Operation Barnabas."

So I applied, and now I was wondering what the hell God had gotten me into.

I first began to sense that this trip wasn't going to go well for me during orientation. I felt like I was being watched all of the time. It was a new feeling. I had always gotten along great with the adults in my life. Peers were another story, but adults and I spoke similar languages. I was overly serious and had spent most of my life surrounded by adult company. As an only child in the care of my grandmother and great-grandmother and mother. As a home-schooled junior and senior high school student, as a kid with a big vocabulary and bigger dreams, adult company had come easy. Not on this trip. From the very first day I felt like I had a target on my back. Maybe it was my baggy clothing and my baseball caps. Maybe it was the way I hung out with certain girls. Maybe there was something in me they could see that I couldn't, and they were determined to stamp it out.

I kept trying to be a team player, but I kept inadvertently failing. During orientation JR, the senior leader, made a big deal about being efficient in the mornings. We were to clean up fast, shower fast, get on the bus, and be ready to go. He bragged about how the shortest shower record ever held was fifteen seconds. I was determined to beat it. I knew I could. One day in the middle of tour, I was ready. In the YMCA locker room, someone readied a stopwatch and I stepped under the water to shower. Thirteen seconds! I was triumphant.

Chapter 2

When I announced it to the leaders it was met with silence, but I was so proud. No one said the fast shower expectation was only for guys, and my desire to win the competition meant I was usurping territory not my own. It happened again when I stood up for one of the women on the tour who was being picked on by some of the guys, and again when I instigated nightly wrestling sessions in the girls' sleeping area. The guys were doing it, so why couldn't we?

And yet I realize I've been set up to fail. In orientation we're in choir practice and the tenors are struggling. There's seventeen guys total in the choir and only four of them. They just can't compete with the volume of the other parts. At the same time, I find myself struggling to sing alto. It's too high for me. When they ask if anyone can sing the tenor part, another alto and I volunteer. I'm relieved because the part is easier to sing and part of me is thrilled because it's something different and I like being different. It'll be fun to be one of the only girls singing tenor. I don't realize that it puts a target on me. Because now I'll be singing with the boys. Me in my short hair and skirt that brushes the floor, in my overlarge denim shirt with the embroidered team logo on it. I've now marked myself as even more different.

ᴗᴗ

"Aren't you a nice young man. I bet you play football!"

I feel my face burn. Rachel is laughing. I don't know how to respond, every answer I can come up with feels wrong, so I just nod. We sing some hymns and then we leave the room.

It's a scene that gets repeated in almost every new place and situation. Older women take my hands, look into my face, and call me a boy. My teammates and I laugh it off together. "Can't they see I'm wearing a skirt?"

Joseph: The Dreamer

When we go to churches, people ask why "that boy" is wearing a skirt. (As if the leaders of Operation Barnabas would ever allow a boy to wear a skirt.) I continue to laugh, but I know there is something in me people are seeing. Something they are reacting to.

Throughout our Sunday morning programs I'm doing all of these skits and dramas that require me to roll on the floor or fall and crawl. Modesty expectations and the skirt I'm required to wear make these dramas difficult, so I ask if I can change into pants or shorts for those skits in order to make them easier. I'm given permission, but once again this difference Others me and I don't realize it. I'm just relieved to have a bit more time not wearing a skirt, a bit more ease of motion, a bit more comfort, but as I sing with the choir, wearing the clothes from the drama skit, I stand out.

At my mid-tour evaluation, the leaders tear into me. They don't like how I dress. They don't like my baseball cap. They think I spend too much time with certain girls on the team. They don't think I'm a team player. They don't think I'm respectful and deferential enough to the leaders. I feel sick. I don't know what to do. I can't change how I dress in the middle of a summer tour when I am living out of a suitcase. I wonder why they don't realize that what they are asking of me is literally impossible. I make the decision to not wear a hat for the rest of the summer, hoping it will at least take some of the pressure off. I feel wounded.

At every moment on this tour, I feel like someone is watching me and waiting for me to fail. I feel like no matter what I do I am somehow failing.

One night Shelly pulls aside one of the other girls to have a conversation. In the course of talking to the girl, Shelly says, "I don't understand why Shannon tries to look like a boy."

When this is relayed to me later, I am livid. I am not "trying" to look like anything. I am trying to be comfortable in my body, trying to get through this hellish summer. People look at me and think I am trying to be defiant or deviant, but I am simply existing.

I have to admit I am rattled. The summer has poked holes in my confidence. Something has shifted inside me and I'm not sure what it's going to be like to see my mom again. To see my youth group and youth leaders. I don't know how to articulate what has happened to me and what it's done to me. I have this sense that I have been irrevocably changed and I don't know what to do with that.

What I am learning on this trip is that my existence is the issue. My existence is the problem. If I want to fit in and if I want to win their approval, I will have to change my existence.

We finally got to the youth conference at the end of our tour. While there were certain responsibilities we would have over the course of the week, the tour was effectively over. I felt so relieved. I could finally breathe deeply and move through my days with no one watching me anymore. I could spend time with whomever I wanted to spend time with.

On the first day of the conference, I heard that the person who is the head of planning was looking for me. I had no idea what to expect. Am I about to be yelled at again? Sent home? Something else?

"I remember that rap that you did at orientation. Will you share it tonight on the main stage?" he asked.

I was blown away. The rap I performed was one I wrote, all about being on fire for Jesus and how this generation was going to be the one to restore the fervor of Christianity. All summer, at every stop, I would look at the order of service and hope I'd see my rap listed. Every time, it wasn't there. Even when we were doing fun youth events or outdoor carnivals, my rap never made it onto the list. And now I was being asked to perform for the entire conference.

I said of course, and then ran to find my beatboxing partner. I also went to the conference store and bought a baseball cap. If I was performing, I was performing it my way, dressed how I wanted to be dressed. That night, as my name was announced, the cheering was so loud the emcee had to stop for it to die down before he could continue. I took the stage and I rapped and danced and let the applause and screams wash over me.

As I came off the stage JR pulled me aside.

"I know you wanted to perform all summer, but see, this is what happens when you are faithful. You get honored."

Something about the way he said it rang hollow to me. As if the entire summer had been a trial to teach me humility. He meant it as a compliment, I think, but something in his words turned my stomach. I drank some water at the fountain before heading back to my seat with my friends.

The conference felt like a high point, a celebration, and yet there was something in me that had been deeply broken by this summer. When I arrived home, I was anxious in ways I hadn't been before. I felt the walls I was putting up but I knew I needed to in order to protect myself. My youth group leaders from home tried to talk to me about the summer but I couldn't find the words. I just told them it was really hard. I felt like I couldn't trust the adults in my life like I once did. Where I used to believe that all of the adults around me were looking out for me, now I understood some of them could and would do damage.

In a moment of weakness on the tour, feeling alone and not knowing where to turn, I had told my mom she could read my journal when I got home. Of course, I took the offer back as soon as I returned home. I had this sense there were things in there that would give me away. Even though now, reading the journal back as an adult, there is so much left out. There were so many experiences and emotions I didn't write down. But there was enough there to blow the cover I didn't fully realize I was trying to keep in place.

Chapter 2

After that summer on OB, I suddenly felt embarrassed when people called me "he" or mistook me for a boy. At the youth conference, I was told there were youth groups who were having debates about whether or not I was gay. It was the first time someone in a church had said that word in relationship to me and I was terrified about what it meant.

Even though I was an avid journaler with stacks of notebooks, their pages filled with every boring thought that crossed my mind, I didn't write about my sexuality. I didn't mention that I didn't know how to make sense of the feelings I was feeling.

In 1997, when I am sixteen, Ellen DeGeneres comes out on her TV show. My family, avid fans of the show, boycott the episode. I remember laughing uproariously in church as the pastor called her "Ellen Degenerate." I agree with everyone else that the show stops being funny after she comes out. Privately, I am heartbroken, even though I don't have words to explain why. Ellen gave me someone to look up to. Ellen had short hair and wore "masculine" clothes and wasn't interested in dating, and before she came out, she gave me hope that my desire to have short hair and wear the clothes I felt comfortable in was normal. She gave me hope I could be a girl who was comfortable. After she came out, I felt anxiety. What did her coming out say about me? Did this mean having short hair and wearing baggy clothes wasn't normal? Was it a sign that I, too, was "degenerate"? I didn't tell anyone about my fears but they weighed on me. They were visceral enough to still reverberate in my body years later even if I didn't trust myself enough to write about them in my high school journal.

When I get to college, people once again get on my case about how I dress. I get tired of the comments, so one morning I decide that I'm going to do something different. I put on a new outfit and I try something new with my hair. It's cut short, but a little longer on the top. I twist the longer sections and put these little clips in. I don't really know what I'm doing, but I'm trying to make an effort.

I feel nervous about my hair, but also a little proud. "See? I can put effort in! I can be normal!" I scan my card to get into chapel (they track our attendance) and go up to one of my friends. She doesn't say anything about my hair. I ask her how it looks and I can tell she doesn't think it looks good. Right away I feel that familiar rush of shame come over me. Again, I have tried and failed to live up to some kind of feminine standard. Another friend teases me about my hair and all I want to do is go right back to my dorm room and crawl into bed, but now I'm stuck in chapel with my hair in these twists and feeling like a fool.

As soon as chapel is over I run back to my dorm and take out the clips. I feel so embarrassed and ridiculous for being embarrassed. "It's just hair clips! Why are you making such a big deal out of this?" I chastise myself, tell myself to get a grip. And yet, I know there is something deeper here, a sense of failure that is about so much more than a few simple hair clips.

No matter what I do, I can't seem to do it right. No matter how I dress or how I present myself to people, I'm always doing it wrong. From the lone earring to my pants to these hair clips, I'm just a failure. Everyone who looks at me sees that failure and judges me for it. They are afraid of me, put off by my failings.

What I couldn't yet articulate, and what no one else was willing to say, was they saw queerness in me and it terrified them. They saw me violating gender norms and didn't know how to handle it. Some of them wanted to protect me by trying to get me to fall in line, and others wanted to punish me for stepping out of line in the first place, but no one knew how to talk about these transgressions, and so they came at me in a wave of unspoken hostility and fear.

My gender identity and expression—even unstated, unnamed, and in many ways unclaimed—was a threat to the social order. I wasn't someone who was out and proud. I wasn't someone who was trying to make a statement. I was simply trying to be myself, and that audacity was met with reproach. My very being threatened to tear the whole social fabric apart somehow. The only way this system worked is if everyone stayed in their place. We were all cogs in the evangelical machine and I was mucking up the works.

But I didn't have a way to make sense of that. I was just a scared kid trying to figure out what the heck was wrong with me and why it seemed like everyone else could see the problem but me.

I put the hair clips back in my drawer and never pulled them out again. I had tried, and I had failed; I didn't want to be humiliated anymore. Yet I carried the shame of those clips (really the attempt and the responses to my attempt) for years. The burning feeling of being looked at and passed over, dismissed because you couldn't get it right. No one even acknowledged how hard it was for me to try, maybe because they didn't know. They didn't understand what it cost to put myself out there like that and I couldn't tell them. I didn't know how.

Queer and trans people move through the world as screens for other's projections. People look at us and project out their own anxieties around sexuality and gender. They project out their own desires that they haven't made peace with (or even admitted to themselves). They project out all of the unnamed and unloved places in their own souls. When that projection hits us, sometimes, simply by being ourselves, we reflect something back at the person projecting. When they see the projection they become deeply enraged, because it shows them a piece of themselves they don't want to acknowledge. It's in these moments queer and trans people become victims of violence or are rejected and shunned.

People project on me their anxieties around sexuality, around gender and gender roles, and around what it means to move through the world with a body assumed to be female. They put on me all of their expectations. They put on me all of their assumptions. Whatever I reflect back to them creates anxiety. Thinking back to my summer on Operation Barnabas, none of us could name it, so we swam in this dance of awkwardness and I felt continually enveloped in shame.

ᴏᴏ

I see some of my own story in the story of Joseph. Joseph of the Bible, yes, and also of Broadway musical fame. Joseph of the fancy coat. Joseph of the complicated masculinity, just like his father, Jacob (which I will discuss in the next chapter). The story of the first patriarchs of Judaism is a story of generational, masculine trauma. Abraham almost sacrifices his son, Isaac. Isaac grows up to favor his more masculine son, Esau, over the effeminate Jacob. Jacob raises twelve sons, but loves one of the youngest, Joseph, best. This preference is probably because Jacob had also been a younger son and also preferred the company of women to the company of men (Gen. 25:27).[1] These complicated men acting out their complications on one another but without ever naming their anxieties give me great comfort. These ancient stories still give us so much truth about our own culture today. Joseph's story in Genesis 37 and 39-48 reveals to me something about my own story.

Joseph is, at the point we're introduced to him, one of the youngest of Jacob's sons. Joseph's older brothers work every day in the field. They care for their family. They do the right things. Then here comes Joseph prancing about, basking in the love of his father, throwing his status as the favorite in their faces.

One wonders if Jacob saw something of himself in Joseph. In the way Joseph moved and talked. In the way he preferred the company of women. In the way he carried himself. Jacob loved his son. I'm sure he loved all of his children, but we know there was something special about Joseph (Gen. 37:3-4). Maybe Joseph's mannerisms triggered Jacob's protectiveness. Maybe he wanted Joseph to feel the love he never felt from his own father. Maybe Jacob was trying to finally break the generational curse that started with Abraham being willing to sacrifice Isaac.[2] Layers of family history all coming to a head with Jacob and Joseph.

Joseph moves through the world knowing he is loved. Knowing he is special. He feels secure to be himself, to show up as all of who he is, partly because of his father's compassion and blessing.

Joseph is cocky and arrogant. One gets the sense he doesn't help out his family as much as he should. While his brothers work and sweat, he sits and tells them about the dreams he had the night before. It's no wonder he is not well loved by his brothers. We can almost forgive them for their anger. Who wouldn't be mad at a younger sibling shirking his responsibilities?

Then there are the dreams. Joseph doesn't have a well-honed sense of preservation, not yet. People telling us their dreams can be annoying enough, but when the dreams are like Joseph's . . . He comes to his brothers and tells them not only what he dreamt of but also what it meant (37:6–9). He was the sun and they were the planets bowing down to him. He would one day be a ruler and they would be his servants. These were not exactly interpretations to win over the family.

Joseph seems oblivious to the feelings he is engendering in others. And why shouldn't he be oblivious? He's a young person, filled with a sense of himself. He is passionate and mouthy. He's a dreamer, both figurative and literal. He knows he's destined for something bigger than this place he's currently in. Bigger than this community, bigger than this working of the fields, bigger than his family. His deep-seated knowing of himself is part of the problem because he doesn't yet have the wisdom to know how to temper it. He doesn't have the social grace to know when he's stepping over the line. While he shouldn't have to hide any of who he is to be loved by his family, like so many of us, he does.

One day his brothers are in the field and Joseph dances out to see them while wearing a long, colorful robe. It's hard to know why, exactly, it was the robe that caused his brothers to snap. Many people have talked about the meaning of this robe. The word used in Hebrew is considered ambiguous, used only one other time (in 2 Sam. 13:18-19) to refer to a garment worn by the virgin daughter of the king. Whether this garment was a dress for a princess or an extravagant gift given to royalty, it angered Joseph's brothers. This garment, combined with the other ways Joseph transgressed gender norms, enraged Joseph's brothers.[3] Whatever the meaning of this particular garment, we do know it was an extravagant gesture from father to son. It was an overtly generous gift given to one of the youngest sons. A son who didn't do any work. The son who hung out with women. The son who told dreams about how much better he was than everyone else. We can almost forgive the brothers' their anger.

Until it turns violent.

The brothers are tired of being made to feel less than, tired of not getting the attention. But they are also deeply offended by Joseph's very being. There is something in him that seems to incite their violence. They decide to kill Joseph (Gen. 37:18-20). Thankfully a cooler head prevails when Reuben, one of the older brothers, intervenes, and the brothers decide to sell him off. They strip him of his garment and tear it, shred it, and pour blood all over it. We can imagine a frenzy of violence toward this object of their anger. Destroying the thing that marked Joseph's difference from them. Not just the item that showed their father's love, but also the item that showed Joseph's queerness.

The brothers go back to their father with the bloodied garment and Jacob assumes his son is dead. His reaction is telling. In Genesis 37:34-35 it says, "Then Jacob tore his clothes, put a simple mourning cloth around his waist, and mourned for his son for many days. All of his sons and daughters got up to comfort him, but he refused to be comforted, telling them, 'I'll go to my grave mourning for my son.' And Joseph's father wept for him." Jacob, the trickster, has been tricked by his own sons. His grief overwhelms him as the child of his heart is now gone.

When I read this story now, in light of my own experiences of gender nonconformity on the Operation Barnabas trip, I believe the anxiety the leaders expressed about my clothing and my behavior is the same anxiety Joseph's brothers put on him. Their anxiety flared about his flamboyance, his sense of himself, his knowledge that he was destined for bigger things. Then when he came out prancing in that many colored coat, draped in his father's love and approval, the brothers snapped.

This anxiety was about more than favoritism and ego, however; it was also about gender expectations. It was the way that effeminate Jacob loved effeminate Joseph. It was that colorful, gender blending coat that sealed the hatred. It was the final straw of Joseph acting differently than the brothers believed he should.

They take their anger out on Joseph, yes, but they destroy that coat. They rip and shred it. They cover it in blood. It's the coat that they take back to their father as proof of what has happened. The gender anxiety finds its focus in the coat, just like the gender anxiety of my leaders found focus in my baseball caps and singular earring. They lashed out at the external items because they were unable or unwilling to name the internal.

ᴖᴖ

Joseph gets carted off into slavery, passed from hand to hand, made to work. He's isolated and alone. Betrayed by the people who should have loved him most in the world and now he wonders if he'll ever get to go home again. Even if he does get to go home, does he even want to? Is there even a home to go back to? Maybe he should just start all over, start a new life in a land where no one knows where he came from. But first he has to survive.

We get the sense Joseph learns to tone it down pretty quickly. He realizes that being noticed is dangerous. Yet he kind of can't help it. No matter where he goes and what he does he seems to get noticed. Whether it's because he does the best work or can interpret dreams, Joseph shines. There is a spark in him he cannot hide and that, deep down, he doesn't want to hide. He knows he's been made for something more than this. Whatever happens to him, whatever troubles befall him, he knows there is something more going on here. He's meant for more. That certainty keeps him alive and moving forward, even when he is punished for telling the truth, even when he is thrown into prison, even when people forget their promises to him. Joseph knows who he is. The spark in him cannot be extinguished. His deep knowledge of himself and his relationship with the Divine is unshakeable. No matter what other people put him through, he continues to be himself. He can't help it. Though other people try to dim his light, though he tries to dim it himself for safety sometimes, his brilliance shines through.

Toward the end of the Joseph story, after he has been elevated to Pharoah's right hand man, after he has solved the problem of the famine and been put in a position to save the very family who had rejected him, in the moment where he has confronted his brothers with his true identity, he says this, "What you intended for evil, God intended for good" (see Gen. 50:20). This is a hard thing to read. For those of us who have been victims of abuse, for those of us who have suffered trauma, it's easy to read this verbalized forgiveness as an excuse for those who wronged us. We hear echoes of all the times we were told God uses hardship to bring us closer. We hear the message of an abusive God who uses people as chess pieces to accomplish whatever is willed. It's important to remember who is saying this. It's Joseph, not his brothers. It's Joseph, not the people who abused him. In this moment Joseph takes back the power of his own narrative. He writes a new ending to his story. He reframes everything that's happened. This can only be done because he's no longer in a place of suffering. He's no longer being abused.

When I think about what I experienced during Operation Barnabas and all of the messages I received about my body and my sexuality while growing up, it's hard to say those things yielded good. Do I believe God used people to abuse me in order to make me stronger? Absolutely not. My horrific summer wasn't part of some grand plan, and yet, my experience that summer did shape me. Who I am today is inextricably bound up in what happened to me on the summer mission trip. My experiences of growing up being assumed female shaped how I move through the world as a man now. The lessons I was taught about my faith and the unlearning I had to do made me tenacious in holding on to faith. Everything I've been through shapes who I am and how I minister.

Could I have gotten here another way? Would I still be the same person without the trauma? I'd like to think yes, but I honestly don't know. What I do know is I am no longer a child at the mercy of confused adults who don't know what to do with me. I am no longer a young person who has to endure the abuse of people in leadership. I am no longer a victim. I am able to write my own story and own my narrative. I can say the evil that was done, I have turned to good.

Joseph's story asks us to confront the ways we lash out at people we don't understand. It asks us to name the ways in which we become oppressors in systems of violence. When have we called a new identity weird because we didn't understand it? When have we lashed out at someone because their freedom threatened the order of the world we needed in place to make sense of things? When have we pushed someone down in order to get ourselves out of prison?

Joseph's story also asks us to consider what might happen if we make space for the dreamers. How many more people might have been saved had Joseph been given a place of leadership sooner? What other creative solutions might have avoided a famine all together? Whose gifts are we continuing to ignore in our communities? Who are we asking to dim their light so as to not make us uncomfortable? What might happen if we allow those lights to shine at full radiance?

Our world and our churches need creative solutions in order to make justice roll down like waters. We need people living and loving at their fullest expression to combat the isolation and loneliness felt in our world. We need passionate dreamers in colorful coats dancing into the fields to show us another way. We need to encourage children who shimmy and shine, who create new words to explain shifting identities, who show us the way forward. Let us refuse to allow anyone to dim their lights or lash out because they don't understand.

Jacob: The Wrestler

start college just a couple of weeks after my summer on Operation Barn-abas. I'm rooming with one of the young women from my team, living with a roommate for the first time in my life. I'm in a freshman girls' dorm and feeling really out of place. I don't know how to handle the energy, the people who feel free to change in front of you, who talk all the time about boys and getting married before they leave college.

I change in the bathroom so no one sees me. I hide my face whenever anyone else changes. I get teased for it, but I instinctively know getting teased is better than people thinking I am looking at them as they get dressed. I still don't entirely have language for what I'm going through, but I intuitively seem to understand how to protect myself.

My journals from my first year and a half of college are marked by emotional storms as I try to figure out where I fit. I don't feel like I fit in at my college. My friend group is almost entirely made up of people I spent that fateful summer with, and when I am with them, I feel pushed back into being the person I was when I was on tour, a person I no longer want to be. Yet I don't entirely know how to make new friends and so I keep getting pulled back into this circle.

My journals are also marked by a spiritual malaise. I don't know how to be close to God. I feel shaken by my experiences over the summer, but I *also feel silly that one eight-week trip had such an impact. Why was I so afraid? Why was my confidence so shaken? I don't know who I can trust or who I can talk to about these feelings, so I pour myself into my journal pages. I stay up too late, sleep my weekends away, and try to make it through.*

Even as I feel like I don't belong at college, home starts to feel more distant as well. My first year in college I talk to my mom all the time. When I am lonely, she is the first person I reach out to. I am excited to go home for every single break and loathe having to come back. After my first summer at home, though, things begin to change. I can no longer slip back into life at home like I never left. My old friends have new friends. Life has moved on without me. Though I don't quite realize it, I am changing as well.

Year two of college starts much the same as year one. New roommate (also from the summer mission trip), same dorm, more old Operation Barnabas teammates starting their educations. Yet there is a definite shift in tone in my journals. I am getting more and more depressed, struggling more to fit in. I write about feeling like I'm "going crazy" over and over again. I try to pray but it doesn't seem to do any good. I berate myself for not taking my faith life seriously enough even as I'm spending several nights a week doing ministry, going to church almost every Sunday, attending chapel, praying, and reading my Bible. None of it feels like enough. I don't feel like I am enough.

A couple months into my second year of college a friend encourages me to get some help. She tells me I need to deal with my issues. I make a list of all of the "issues" I think I have. There are eighty-one items on the list. I make an appointment with the on-campus counselor. It feels silly and I don't want to talk to a stranger, but my friends have had enough of my depression and rambling. I sense if I don't call this counselor I'm going to be even more alone.

In hindsight I don't blame my friends (though I did at the time). When you grow up in an evangelical church setting, you're quite sheltered. Most of us were seventeen and eighteen but had the life experience of thirteen-year-olds. My friends, even the ones who had gone to public school, didn't know how to deal with someone who was in severe emotional pain. We were also taught anything could be solved by prayer and if you had an issue that wasn't being resolved you were probably doing something wrong. It's no wonder they looked at me and made judgments and assumptions. It's no wonder they weren't equipped to actually walk with me in my depression.

At the time I felt abandoned. I felt like no one wanted me around; I was bringing everyone down. I felt like I was being pushed to the side or told I wasn't welcome until I could be happy like them. I felt like I was too much for everyone in my life. Everyone left me eventually; my father, my stepfather, my friends. Maybe I wasn't worth sticking around for; maybe being alone was my lot in life. Everything I saw around me confirmed the feelings of despair. It was isolating and alienating.

When I told my mom I was going to see the counselor she was hurt. She asked, "Why can't you just talk to me about things?"

I couldn't explain it to her. I needed someone else to talk to. She brought up the counseling several times, almost always with a tone of disapproval. She wanted me to talk only to her about what I was feeling. This rift in our relationship would continue to grow.

I made the appointment and saw the counselor. I went for a couple of weeks until one week she brought up something about how I dressed. She mentioned that I hid my femininity. I felt put on the spot, but also like she had gotten it wrong. I wasn't trying to hide anything; I was trying to be myself. I couldn't articulate my sense of self or of gender, so I immediately shut down. The next week I accidentally slept through my appointment and I never made another one. My first foray into counseling was over.

During my first year of college, I had befriended two upperclassmen. I'm not sure how we met; I think one of them might have played on the softball team. I was the manager because I wasn't good enough to get a spot even on the bench. These two women were fun and funny. They put me at ease. They were physically affectionate with one another and I remember thinking, "Finally. Other people like me." I felt like I could be myself with them. Shortly after we met and started hanging out, they were both expelled from the college for being lesbians. I was shocked and hurt. I was also afraid. Afraid, once again, of what seeing myself reflected in them said about me. Afraid that people would come after me, too. I also knew that anything I told the counselor that violated the school's very intense and exhaustive lifestyle code could be reported, so when the counselor brought up how I dressed, everything flashed through my head at once and I shut down in order to protect myself. I had the sense that if we really delved into what was at the core of my issues everything would unravel. She would report me to student affairs, I would be expelled, and my life would be over.

This deep sense of fear was paralyzing. I didn't know where to put it. I didn't have anyone to talk to about it. It felt like everyone was just waiting for you to slip so they could report you and get you into trouble. Students at my college got punished for all sorts of things: drinking, smoking cigarettes, and even dancing at their own weddings. It felt like we walked around just waiting to be called into an office to be reprimanded. As someone who hates having people be unhappy with me, I was terrified all the time. I had visions of getting kicked out and having to explain it to my mom and church and getting kicked out of those places, too. I couldn't cope with that possibility, so I just did my best to follow all of the rules. I didn't smoke or drink. I made it back to the dorm by curfew. I tried to not do anything illicit. Yet, I often felt that simply by existing I was breaking some kind of rule.

I didn't realize until years later that the level of fear I was experiencing wasn't normal. I was afraid all of the time and I had been almost all of my life. Most of my fear started much earlier than college, when my grandmother died. I started my life as the only child of a single mother who had just moved back home to live with her parents. Grandparents, mother, and child all living together under the same roof. As my mom worked full time, I would spend the days with my grandmother, whom I called Grandmom. As I got older we would sit and talk. I sat for hours on her lap sucking my thumb while she held me. She had cancer and was dying. I knew she was sick. On the night that Grandmom died, I remember praying before bed that she wouldn't die. I woke up in the middle of the night and she was gone. I was allowed to go to her, to sit on the bed with her body. Then someone made me tea with milk and sugar and I drank it and went back to bed. Rooted in my thinking thereafter was this: "If you ask God to do something, God will do the opposite." I started to be more cautious with my prayers.

I accepted Jesus as my "personal Lord and Savior" when I was four or five years old, shortly after my grandmother died. I was asking about where she was and I was told that she was in heaven, so of course I wondered where I was going to go. My mom told me about heaven and hell. About Jesus's death on the cross. About how if I didn't accept Jesus into my heart I would go to hell and be separated from God and my grandmother for all eternity. Of course, I didn't want that. I was so scared. I felt the weight of eternity, that long, long time without Grandmom. I prayed to accept Jesus and my mother rejoiced. I was happy that she was happy. I was happy I wasn't going to hell.

The fear didn't go away, though; it just warped and morphed. I was afraid I hadn't prayed the right prayer, or I hadn't really meant it. I was afraid I wasn't actually saved. I was afraid the Rapture (an event when all true Christians will be taken to heaven by Jesus, or so I was taught) was going to happen and I was going to be left behind. I was afraid if I didn't witness to other people enough and they didn't believe in Jesus they would die and go to hell and it would be all my fault. I was afraid I wasn't serious enough about my faith. I was afraid Jesus was going to come back before I had the chance to grow up and I was also afraid that being afraid of Jesus coming back meant I wasn't a good Christian and therefore God would smite me. I was afraid that not wanting to wash people's feet meant I wasn't living out my faith correctly. A litany of fears kept me awake at night. I would lie in my bed and think about eternity and how long eternity was and worry about getting bored just praising God for eternity and worry that worrying about getting bored probably meant I wasn't saved and what if I went to hell for eternity instead and suffered and suffered and then my brain would finally shut down and I would drift off.

At least once a year we would hear a sermon about the horrors of the crucifixion and about how the excruciating torture Jesus experienced was all for us. Our wretchedness put Jesus on the cross. We deserved what they did to Jesus, but he took our place. As a child who was very concerned with doing the right things—being obedient and respectful, making my mother happy, following the rules— these guilt laden sermons made me feel awful. I was trying so hard to be good, but I kept messing up. I would lose my temper or tell a fib. I would disobey or accidentally be disrespectful. Over and over again I felt the guilt for killing Jesus. For being so awful that God couldn't even look at me without Jesus standing between us.

To me, God was capricious. God was a bit of a bully. God would brutalize and kill Jesus for someone else's sin. God would take my grandmother away from me. God would send a child to hell for not praying the right prayer, so I needed to figure out how to not make God mad at me. If I could just do that then I would be okay. I wouldn't pray for outrageous things anymore. I would read my Bible and go to church. I would figure out how to get through foot washing. I would believe and believe correctly. I would make God happy, just like I had to make my mom happy, just like I had to make my pastors happy, and all of the other adults in my life.

I never stopped to ask if making other people happy was the right way to live. I never considered my views of God to be anything other than correct. I was a child who believed everything I had been taught. No wonder I was already afraid.

ᗧᗧ

Sophomore year of college, at least the first two-thirds, was the hardest period of my life. I would spend hours just staring at the wall. I couldn't focus, but I also couldn't rest. I would drive somewhere and just sit. Other times a sort of primal rage would overtake me when I was alone and I would punch the cement walls in our dorm room until my knuckles bled and my wrist hurt. I didn't know where to put my anguish, so I took it out on myself. From reading through my old journals now, I realize I was having panic attacks and didn't know it. Several times I thought I was having a heart attack: my chest would hurt and I would feel like I couldn't breathe. I didn't know who to call, who to reach out to, so I suffered alone and wrote another entry in my journal.

Something had to give, but I didn't know what. My best friend from high school got married and we talked less and less. My friends in college didn't know what to do for me or how to make space for me to show up as I was, and so I found myself floundering. I hung out with people but that often left me feeling worse about myself. I took solace in my journal, in having a space where I could say what I wanted to say without fear of judgment or recrimination. I started to open up a bit more; before that year I had been afraid to even write about my sexuality, afraid that talking about it made it real, but not talking about it made me unable to cope. It's in that year that I started to mention "struggling with homosexuality." I talked about people perceiving me as gay and not knowing what to do. It was very clear to me I was alone in this struggle and I needed to deal with it on my own. When I revealed even a bit of myself, people met me with caution and fear, so I stopped revealing myself, at least for a bit.

I kept auditioning for theater pieces and I kept getting rejected. It felt like everything I had built my identity around was getting stripped away. I came into college determined to be a contemporary Christian music star. I was going to be a singer/songwriter and devote my life and ministry to telling people about Jesus through song. In my first year of college I performed anywhere people would have me: coffee houses, church basements, the student union. I recorded songs in my dorm room on a karaoke machine that recorded cassettes. I wrote songs and played them for anyone who would listen, but as I entered my second year, I got this sense I wasn't going to make it as a music star. I didn't have the talent, and slowly the drive to succeed in that arena was leaving me. Without my passion I was adrift. A friend told me I needed to find a new passion, somewhere else to put my creative energy. She was right, but I didn't know where to put it. Not quite yet.

I took a class called "Religious Drama Workshop." The semester-end assignment was to write several short plays or a one-act play. I chose the one-act. It was like all of the church drama skits I wrote in high school, but on a larger scale. I started to see the beauty of being able to tell longer, more complicated stories. My one-act was about a group of friends who were trying to get through life. In some ways it was inspired by my newfound obsession with *RENT*.

I discovered the musical *RENT* from someone who gave a speech about it in one of our public speaking classes. I had never heard of it before and I was captivated by this idea of people living and loving in New York. I was also intrigued by someone at my Christian college talking about a musical production that dealt with gay people. And so, on my next trek to Walmart, I picked up the *Selections from RENT* CD. I didn't really understand how cast albums worked and so I didn't know that by buying the selections, I was leaving out a massive part of the musical. I listened to the CD and was mostly confused. I had no idea how this story fit together or what happened between the songs, but something in the music spoke to me. It was the first time since the Ellen incident that I had a bit of a touchstone for people that were maybe like me.

I wanted to basically write a Christian *RENT* as a one-act. I packed as many issues into this short play as I could; abusive parents, teen pregnancy, eating disorders, and suicide. I handled them all badly, having had no experience with any of them other than the depression. Yet, even as I wrote a piece far outside of my ability, I realized I could use art and writing to grapple with questions and ideas. Every piece I created didn't need to have all of the answers. I didn't need to present the story of Jesus at the end. No one needed to "get saved." It felt like a revelation. Art could do something different, something more. It could give me a new outlet for my passions.

I got permission to turn the one-act into a full-length play and offer it as a student-led production in the campus theater. I was thrilled. Suddenly I had a new place to put my energy. As I became more and more invested in this piece, the process also gave me something else: an entirely new friend group.

Theater saved me in ways I didn't understand back then. Having a place to ask my questions, having a group of friends who—for once—never said a word about how I dressed or how short my hair was, and having something to look forward to and invest energy into felt like a miracle. But the real miracle came when we performed the play. We scheduled one weekend of three performances, and that was it. The theater was packed. People were sitting on the floors and in the aisles. No one wanted to miss this. The response was incredible, both the sheer number of people there, and also the emotional response. This was different from another 1930s murder mystery being depicted on stage. This was a play talking about real issues, hard topics. People saw themselves on the stage; they were able to feel not so alone. When people told me they felt seen by my words, I, in turn, felt seen.

I realized theater could be a helpful feedback loop. I could ask questions, wrestle with hard things, put myself into these works, share all of the places where I felt alone and vulnerable, and then when people watched my plays, we would both realize we weren't alone after all; we were in this together. Life-changing realization.

Theater helped to pull me out of my crippling depression. It gave me a new focus and purpose. Of course, it also brought new stress and complications because we were in college and immature and juggling too much with insufficient emotional resources. But even in the midst of the new challenges, I was finally finding my footing.

I had a home in the Communications department, taking every class I could for my major, being a Teacher's Assistant for several semesters of Public Speaking, investing myself in learning and growing. Frank, the head of the department and my favorite professor, gave me a safe place to struggle. He encouraged hard questions in his classes, and he encouraged divergent thought. He wanted us to grapple and question and not just give the "right" answer. In his classes I felt my brain come alive. I was often the outlier, bringing up the things people didn't want to see, but he encouraged me when

I did so. And when I showed up to class looking like hell, he sent me home and told me to rest. He was compassionate and kind and I desperately needed an adult like that in my life. I will remain forever grateful for the ways in which he stepped up for me. When I came back to visit the college a couple of years after graduation, I told him I was gay. He affirmed me and said nothing negative. It was a balm to my weary and harassed soul.

Theater, Frank, and my new friends got me through my last years at college. I finally felt like I had a place to belong. The problem was that belonging with these particular people, embracing this newfound desire to question and struggle, meant that going home was harder and harder. I was no longer satisfied with easy answers. I was no longer satisfied with "believe it because we say it." I wanted to understand *why*. My (now) lifelong practice of looking around and asking, "Who is there not space for?" kept coming back, and the answer was a whole lot of people. There wasn't space for people who asked questions. Who didn't toe the line. Who struggled. Who weren't happy all the time. Who thought there might be something more. I wanted to create space for those people; I wanted to create space for myself.

When you start to stand up to a closed system, the system tries to smack you back into place. I started to receive critical comments on my theology papers, such as, "Your subjective view of Scripture concerns me." I realized that the professors in a lot of my classes didn't want to encourage us to think; they wanted us to just believe what they thought were the "right" answers. My systematic theology class was the worst. The professor would bring up a theological claim, like salvation or the nature of God. He would offer two different views from Christian history and thought and explain why they were wrong. Then he would offer his view and lecture about why it was the only right one. The entire point of the class wasn't to help us to figure out theology; it was to indoctrinate us.

As I entered my senior year of college, I was no longer willing to be indoctrinated. A lifetime of being told what to think and believe, how to act, how to dress—it was all starting to chafe. As much as I had always been my own person and done my own thing, I was still entangled in systems of thought that I had previously just accepted. I could no longer just accept anything someone in authority said. As I came more and more to terms with my sexuality, I realized that I couldn't take anything for granted anymore. If I was going to survive (and I mean that literally), I was going to have to think for myself. If I was going to keep my faith intact, if I was going to make sense of my life and my identity, I was going to have to question everything I had been taught and figure out my own answers. I could no longer just believe what I had been told to believe; I needed to actually believe it for myself.

This felt incredibly risky. What if I couldn't find answers that I could live with? What if other people couldn't live with my answers? I struggled with whether I was just deceiving myself (the church I grew up in certainly thought I was). What if there was no way for me to be myself and hold on to my faith?

There were moments when I wanted to walk away from Christianity. It felt easier. It felt like leaving everything behind would be a lot better than trying to integrate what I was coming to know about myself with what I had been taught. And yet, I didn't feel I could leave it behind. Even when I took a break—I stopped going to church for a while, dropped out of leading youth groups, and took a breather from prayer and reading the Bible—I still had a sense that there was something in this Jesus story that was calling me back. There was something about God that I couldn't seem to shake. I didn't understand this sense then, because in the moment it felt like God was making me miserable. I wondered if God was punishing me.

I grew up hearing my mother and my pastors pray that God would break someone's heart to bring them back into the fold. I had heard people say that sometimes God needs to break us to make us. I believed that if I stepped too far out of line God might smite me to bring me back. I grew up believing in a bully God who would torture his son just because he couldn't look upon sinful people. If God was willing to torture his perfect son, then what would God be willing to do to me, an imperfect human? God was someone to be terrified of. God was mercurial and would make bad things happen in order to make you behave rightly. Asking questions of this God was a risky business.

So, I wondered, was all of my experience Stockholm syndrome? Could I not leave Christianity because I thought God would kill me? That may have been part of it, but I also had this sense that I was meant to do something in the church. I was meant to do something for God. I had this idea that God could use even me. But I had to figure out what I believed first. I had to figure out who I was and what my relationship with God could look like.

I didn't have any examples to follow outside of my small Christian community. I didn't know any mainline or liberal Christians. I must have had some idea that they existed "out there" somewhere, but I also didn't think much of their faith. I was convinced that we had the right theology and that everyone else was misguided and wrong. I swallowed all of the lies that said that only fundamentalist evangelicals could know real peace and love.

I worried a lot about my depression because I was taught that Christians, real Christians, understood joy. I was not joyful. I was terrified. I was lonely. I was sad. I did not have the "peace that passes understanding." And yet I knew that I believed in Jesus and God. I knew that I was "saved." I may have doubted occasionally, but I knew in my heart of hearts that I was a Christian. So, what was I doing wrong? Why didn't I feel the joy I was supposed to feel? We didn't talk about mental health in my church. We didn't make space for people with depression and mental illness. No one ever encouraged me to consider medication. My college therapist mentioned it once in our initial meeting, but it never came up again. I didn't know about or understand chemical imbalances. I didn't know that stress impacted your health. I just thought I wasn't praying enough or reading my Bible enough. I thought I could will myself to be better, that all of my problems were the cause of my own sin and unwillingness to just try harder.

This was a potent combination: depression, coming to terms with sexuality, starting to question the faith I had been raised in, all while still being completely immersed in a conservative evangelical world. I had no real outlet. I had no friends who weren't Christian. I didn't think you could have authentic relationships with people who didn't believe the way that you did, so any potential friends who weren't "saved" were seen as a mission field. As people to potentially convert. My college journals are filled with misguided attempts to witness to people, with phrases like "a seed was planted," which I now understand probably meant that I (1) pissed someone off with my proselytizing or (2) made light of their struggle by telling them to turn to Jesus to make it better. It is a wonder anyone still talked to me at all after those clumsy sessions. I didn't understand anything about how the world worked. I was closed off to actual life because I had never experienced it. Everything was theoretical.

But every once in a while, it seemed like a bit of clarity emerged. I was able to confide in some people at college that I "struggled with homosexuality," and instead of being condemned, I was invited to share more of my struggle. I finally felt like I didn't have to keep everything so tightly wrapped up. I was able to share a bit more of myself. The relief was immeasurable, but tinged with fear. I worried the wrong people would find out. I worried word would get out and I would get expelled. Even though I hadn't done anything "gay," I still feared that even admitting my struggle put me at risk for expulsion. Not to mention my terror that my mother would find out. I knew she wouldn't understand, so I had to do everything in my power to keep this information from her.

I was starting to realize that much of the closeness I felt with my mother was predicated on us being in lockstep: on beliefs, on religious practices, on emotional connection. As soon as I started to become out of step with her, the closeness became complicated. A push pull started. Questions were asked that had only one right answer, which I struggled to give, and when my answers didn't elicit her satisfaction, I would be met with a lecture as to why I was wrong, even if I had firmly considered my thinking.

The more I read and learned, the harder it became to keep believing the things I had grown up believing. I was going to have to make some decisions. If I could no longer believe in the faith that had been handed to me, then I was going to have to find a faith of my own. My faith in that final year of college felt like a house of cards. I worried if I bumped the table it was sitting on the whole thing would crash down around me, and yet the rumbles were already starting. The ground I was standing on was shifting and quaking. The house was tottering.

Strangely enough, the first card to fall wasn't the card about homosexuality. It wasn't the card about gender. It was the card about the Rapture.

In the faith tradition of my youth, the Rapture was a big deal. It was also a big business with everything from hit songs ("I Wish We'd All Been Ready" by Larry Norman, made famous by dc Talk), to books (the bestselling *Left Behind* series), to movies (based on those books and starring Kirk Cameron and featuring a host of cameos from contemporary Christian music artists. My favorite is an incredibly out of place and underdressed Bob Carlisle of "Butterfly Kisses" fame saying,

"That's our Buck!" in an odd Southern drawl). I grew up believing that the Rapture was going to happen any day. If there was ever a moment where I couldn't find my family, I worried that I had been left behind. I devoured the *Left Behind* books and wondered if I would have the courage of the heroes on these pages. Could I withstand torture, or would I give in and be sent to eternal damnation?

The Rapture was considered a given. We all believed it. It was "what the Bible taught." It was handed down to us practically from Jesus, right? Turns out this was very wrong. I was reading Bruce Bawer's book *Stealing Jesus: How Fundamentalism Betrays Christianity* and he has a section on the Rapture. It wasn't something the earliest Christians taught and believed. In fact, the idea didn't come about until the late 1800s, in England, by a man named John Nelson Darby. I was in shock. This doctrine that had terrified me my entire life, this doctrine that made me feel shame and fear, this doctrine that caused so much anxiety, was invented by an English dude two hundred years ago? Are you kidding me? I put the book down and thought, "If they lied to me about this, what else have they lied to me about?"

Some people would say that's a harsh response. They weren't lying to me; they were just teaching what they believed. But not a single person ever taught me where this idea of the Rapture came from. No one ever traced it back to its source. It was simply assumed that if they believed it, it came from the Bible and everyone believed it. But here I was, reading that book (and not even an academic book, a popular book!) and the author was telling me the truth. What else had been kept from me? The more I read, the more the house of cards I had been believing in started to come down. Were there even more ways to understand other theological ideas that had troubled me? This one question brought down the house. That's the thing about certain strands of evangelical theology: every piece depends on every other piece being true. You stack card after card, and you desperately try to hold the table steady. But when you bump the table, when you ask the first question, when you pull the first card of belief out of the house, the whole thing comes down. It's why they didn't want me to ask all of those questions. It's why we were encouraged to just trust, just believe.

I stood before an imaginary table with an entire deck of cards flattened and on top of each other. It was terrifying, yes, but it was also freeing. I could, for the first time, hold each card up to the light and examine it. I could weigh it on its own merits. Each belief and idea no longer depended on the one next to it, which meant I could chase it down to its source. I could ask all of the hard questions. I could turn a card, and turn it again, and decide whether to include it in my new house or discard it if it was too damaged to play a healthy role.

Even as I sat with my scattered deck of cards, I still had the table. The foundation. I believed, still, in the Christian story. I wanted to be a part of the church. I wanted to follow Jesus. Even as I was questioning everything, that much I was sure of. At least most days.

My quest for answers became insatiable. I started to realize that there were entire swaths of theology no one had told me about. All of those "right" ideas and "one way to understand this passage" were fundamentally untrue. There were decent, smart, educated Christians who believed the exact opposite. There was an entire world of understandings on many of those foundational passages.

I realized, too, that some of my pastors must have known there were other ideas and understandings about these theological tenets. They went to seminary, they read books by other theologians, yet they chose to tell us there was only one way to believe.

I started to read everything I could get my hands on. I started to allow myself to ask all of the questions that had been percolating in my mind but that I felt I wasn't allowed to ask: Did Jesus really have to die? Isn't a God who demands a blood sacrifice kind of abusive? Did everyone who didn't pray a certain prayer really go to hell for all eternity? Were there other ways to understand the end times? What did the "kingdom of God" really mean? The questions tumbled and rolled and I read and read and read.

My house of cards had fallen around me, and I simply let it be. I didn't try to build up the remains, not yet; I just left it all apart. I wanted to see what would be left when my questions had answers. If I razed the entire house, would there be a foundation to build something new on? I wasn't sure, but I knew that my mental and spiritual health depended on seeing where this whole process of discovery led. I could no longer keep shoving my questions down. I could no longer just accept what I had been told to believe without figuring it out for myself. I had to have satisfying answers.

Right after college graduation, I was reading *If Grace Is True: Why God Will Save Every Person* by James Mullholland and Philip Gulley. The book talks about other ways to understand the life, death, and resurrection of Jesus. Instead of being about Jesus dying to secure heaven for us, the authors talked about empire and standing up for what's right. They talked about God not as a punitive father that demanded blood, but as someone who grieved the death of Jesus. They talked about salvation not as a get-out-of-hell-free card, but as participation in the work of God. I was captivated. It made sense to me in a way that the "getting saved" messages I had been taught my whole life never had. It also felt healthy. Suddenly salvation wasn't about trying to appease an abusive heavenly father; it was about expressing gratitude and receiving grace and participating in the work of salvation. Honestly, believing in this kind of salvation required more of me than the "pray a prayer and go to heaven" theology ever did.

My mom saw *If Grace Is True* on my floor and wasn't happy.

"If there's no hell, why did Jesus have to die?"

That was, indeed, the question I was trying to answer. But her response to the book taught me two things: (1) the idea that there might be another way to understand salvation was so foreign she thought it needed to be completely rejected out of hand; (2) reading certain books could shake our faith and so we should avoid those books. I thought, "If my faith can be shaken by reading a book, maybe it means my faith wasn't so solid in the first place."

I didn't know it then, but this grappling I was doing with my faith, this wrestling, not only has precedent in Scripture but is held up as one of the most faithful things you can do.

⌒⌒

In Genesis 25:26, we're introduced to Jacob. From the very beginning he's named as a troublemaker. The second-born twin who tries to beat his brother out of the birth canal. The twin who comes out grasping his brother's heel. Then he becomes the young man who prefers the company of his mother and the kitchen over the more "proper" male pursuits of hunting and fieldwork, who grows into a "quiet man living in tents" (25:27).

His mother favors him, but his father offers only contempt. I wonder sometimes how the trauma of Abraham almost sacrificing Isaac stayed with Isaac. How did it impact how he treated his own sons? Was he ever able to get out from under the weight of the knowledge that God was more important to his father than he was?

We get the sense that from a very young age Jacob knows that he's going to have to take care of himself. He gets his brother to trade his birthright for a bowl of soup (25:29–34). We're supposed to see this as a horrible, nasty thing for Jacob to do, but no one ever seems to talk about how callous Esau was in his disregard for that birthright. Why was he so willing to trade it away? Maybe he didn't think Jacob was serious, or he thought he was so strong he could take it back by force. Maybe he mistook Jacob's gentleness for weakness and, like so many rough men, believed he could simply have whatever he wanted without working for it. Yet, later in life, Jacob is the one named a trickster in the text, a cheater, taking what isn't his to take (27:35-36).

I wonder if Jacob knew how hard his life was going to be and so he was taking out whatever insurance policies he could to protect himself. And his mother, Rebekah, plotted to help him. After the incident with the bowl of soup and the birthright, the twins' father is nearing his death. Isaac plans to bestow a blessing on Esau, his favored son. We don't know if he knew about Esau trading away his birthright. If he did, maybe Isaac believed he could make things right, give Esau a special blessing that would even things out between the brothers again.

In Genesis 27:1-29, we see the narrative unfold. Rebekah comes to Jacob with a plan. A woman in the company of men. A woman—probably used to being told what to do, being robbed of her agency, and seeing how rough the world was being with her gentle son—decides to claim some agency for them both. She helps Jacob impersonate his brother and go to his father to claim that blessing. His father suspects something when Jacob speaks. What is it in his voice that gives him away? Was it his articulation? An effeminate way of speaking? A certain turn of phrase? But when Isaac feels the hair on his arms (the wool of a sheep repurposed for just that moment) and smells the musk of the field, he goes on with the blessing anyway. Possibly Isaac didn't think enough of the intelligence of Jacob and Rebekah to be able to trick him. He offers the blessing and Jacob takes it.

Esau finds out and is furious (27:30-41). Once again, he is being robbed of something he believes that he deserves. That was supposed to be his blessing. He wants to kill Jacob. And once again, Rebekah intervenes (27:42-26). She tells Jacob to run, but then she also goes to Isaac and asks him to send Jacob away. To send him back to her family so that he can find a better wife than the ones Esau has married. It's another insurance policy because if Isaac has sent Jacob away, Esau shouldn't chase him. Jacob leaves. He flees with the things he can carry. He leaves with his mother's help. He doesn't do the manly thing and stay and fight. He doesn't stand up for himself. He doesn't try to claim his space. He just goes.

On his first night alone Jacob has a dream (28:10-17). The dream is of a ladder stretching from the earth into heaven, angels ascending and descending, and he receives a promise that he will be blessed. That he will be given land and children. That he will become a mighty nation. Before this, the text doesn't mention anything about Jacob and God. This is the first time that God speaks to Jacob and it's when he's alone. When he finally gets away from the plotting and scheming of his family, he's able to connect with the Divine and hear a word of goodness spoken on his life.

Jacob wakes up and goes on his way, continuing to trick and cheat his way through the world. Sure, there are reversals, like when his uncle Laban tricks Jacob into marrying his older daughter, Leah, first instead of Rachel, the daughter Jacob really desires (29:15-30). Jacob settles for a while. Working for his wives, then having child after child (29:31-30:24). His wives compete with one another for his affection, and even as son after son after son is born to Leah, we don't get the sense that Jacob is swayed away from his love of Rachel. Is there something about all of this masculinity coming from someone who is not connected to his own masculinity that shakes him?

After many years, Jacob becomes restless. His family is growing, but he still feels unmoored. One senses that he is playing some kind of long game as he gets his revenge on Laban by selectively breeding sheep to claim himself a vast herd before, once again, running away. It's framed in the story as a mutual leave-taking, but the undercurrent is that if Jacob doesn't leave on his own, Uncle Laban is going to force the issue. The time of mutual advantage taking is over. Jacob knows how to read a room; his survival has depended on it. He always knows how to protect himself and so he goes taking everything and everyone he has amassed with him. Adrift and roaming again (30:25–31:55).

Word comes to him that his brother Esau is looking for him and wants to see him (32:6). Had Jacob had any interactions with his family of origin since he left? Had he talked to his mother? Told her of his marriage and his children? Or had he been completely cut off from communication?

Jacob decides to meet with Esau. Maybe he was tired of running. Tired of the worry that dogged his every move. Tired of feeling like he can't just claim the things that are his but that he needs to keep fighting and scraping for a place. Maybe he just wants to get the whole ordeal over with. But he's not going down without being smart about it. He splits his family apart so that he can come to Esau without appearing like he's a threat. He sends gifts ahead of him to flatter his brother (32:7–21).

The night before the meeting Jacob sends everyone away from him and he is alone. There is a sense that he needs this time to prepare himself. Maybe he wants to commune with God. Or simply to not have to be around other people. Maybe he wants to practice the speech he will give when he sees his brother. He manages to fall asleep, and once again, alone in the wilderness, he is visited by the Divine. A figure who comes and wrestles with him (32:24–32 covers

67

the rest of the story). Jacob clings to this person. They grapple with one another all through the night. It's an image of violence, yes, but also of tenderness. Anyone who has watched mixed martial arts fighting knows that there are moments in the midst of the struggle when the two fighters only have the strength to cling to one another, and almost by agreement, simply rest in one another's arms. A fight that lasted all night long must have had several of these moments of resting. Jacob and the stranger, holding one another. Feeling their hearts beat hard together. Sweat mingling, breath tickling in each other's ear. It's surprisingly intimate.

It's the reason I got involved in the wrestling matches during Operation Barnabas. I wanted to grapple, but more than anything I wanted to hold and be held. I wouldn't have been able to say that out loud. I couldn't ask for what I needed, but I knew, deep in a place without words, that I longed for connection and closeness. And I also knew that I couldn't seem to get it any other way than by fighting for it.

The story of Jacob wrestling with the angel became a touchpoint for me.

When we read Jacob's story, we don't get the sense that he has a strong relationship with the Divine. It's not like Abraham's story where every other day he's having a conversation with God. Making and breaking promises. Being told where to go and how to live. Jacob has two direct encounters with God: both happen at night, both happen when he is alone. One comes in a dream and one comes in the form of a wrestling partner. And yet there is something about Jacob that God pays attention to. There is something in him that God wants to use.

This moment of wilderness wrestling is captivating. Jacob wrestles with the stranger and refuses to let go. He clings in a way he has never clung before. In the past when Jacob was at risk he cut and ran. But this time, he stays. He holds on. He says, "I will not let you go unless you bless me" (32:26b). What a statement.

As my faith unraveled during my Christian college experience, I returned to this story of Jacob wrestling. There was something about Christianity that I couldn't let go of, even though I desperately wanted to. I was tired. Worn out. I'd been wrestling now for years. With God, with my identity, with my family, with the Bible. Couldn't I just let go? Couldn't I just walk away? And yet I continued to cling. There was something in me that was fighting for the blessing, believing that there was indeed one for me. There was more in my story. There was more in my faith. There was more in my relationship with God than simply a set of rules that I could never seem to live up to. There had to be. I had to believe that God could bless me. That somehow, I could cling to my faith.

Jacob wrestles until dawn, refusing to let go. The man he is wrestling with realizes that this isn't going to end and something has to shift, so he strikes Jacob in the hip. He wounds him, but then he gives him a blessing. Jacob releases his grip.

The wounding, the blessing, the release.

The wounding, the blessing, the release.

Then a new name.

The wrestling partner announces that Jacob is now to be called Israel (32:28). He is to become the father of a new nation. A nation named after his changed name.

Ever after, Israel walks with a limp. He limps to meet his brother, and maybe this newfound humility is what causes Esau to fall on Jacob's neck and forgive him. Maybe it's this limp that endears him to his family.

When I was younger, I would pray God would fix me, make me normal so I could fit back into the world I came from. What I didn't realize until reflecting more on Jacob's story is that my wounding meant that going home, going back to the way things were before, was impossible. I was going to be forever changed. Remade, even if not renamed.

CHAPTER 4

Rahab: The Sexual Outsider

Growing up, I had this idea that queer people were sex-crazed freaks who were ruled by their hormones and desires. They got AIDS because they couldn't behave themselves. Every single homosexual on the planet was an addict and depressed. There was no such thing as a moral gay person; the presence of homosexual desires proved how depraved and disgusting gay people were. Don't even think about there being a happy gay person. People made jokes about how the word "gay" used to mean happy, but now it meant something perverted. Gay people's diseases and unhappiness were all punishments from God because of their sickness.

I internalized the idea that being gay was basically all about sex, even though that wasn't my experience once I started to understand my sexuality. My desire was for relationship, intimacy, connection. Because my desire was for women, though, I internalized the belief that there was something distorted in me. Something sick and sinful. Something deeply twisted.

I heard people claim that gay people did a lot of drugs and drank a ton. They had orgies and lots and lots of sex, most of it hidden and shameful. They also flaunted their sexuality all over the place! (My young mind didn't grasp the contradiction between having hidden sex and flaunting one's sexuality.) Even though I didn't do drugs or even touch alcohol or have orgies (or even want to be a part of orgies), I thought there must be some truth in these claims. After all, if this is what people believed, certainly that's the way it is, right? There were studies after all! Statistics! Research!

I also read about the increased rate of depression and suicidality in gay people. Authors and "experts" posited that being gay is what made you depressed. You were depressed because deep down you knew you were living in a depraved way. The popular wisdom among adults in my church and the studies they cited painted a picture of a sick subculture. One of lies and deception. Of addiction and mental health issues. Of disease and brokenness.

In the closed system of American evangelicalism, it all made a kind of sick sense. They could talk you in circles until you were so turned around that you accepted what they said as a gospel truth. Correlation and causation. Cause and effect. But there was so much more to the story once you knew how to look at the data differently.

We never talked about how when you live in a hostile world, you have to find ways to cope. We didn't talk about how when your sexuality is considered illegal then any sex act becomes illicit, even monogamous sex between people in long-term relationships. We didn't talk about how when most people call you depraved and disgusting, when you are ridiculed and reviled, when you can and do get kicked out of your house or fired from your job for coming out, that rejection might, just might, impact your mental health and make you depressed and suicidal. We didn't talk about the potential causes, just the effect.

I was taught that it wasn't the church's fault that these gay people were so depressed, of course; even if it was, they got what they deserved because they were depraved. See how the reasoning works? Circular logic. Twists and turns and excuses to tie people up in knots. The bottom line? Gay people = bad.

Years later, in college and just after, when I realized my desire for women wasn't going away no matter how hard or long I prayed and that God didn't seem to be "fixing me," I became determined to at least buck the trends. I wasn't going to do drugs or become an alcoholic. I wasn't going to indulge in inappropriate sex. I wasn't going to flaunt anything. I was going to be a pure, modest, abstinent person. Just gay. I could have all of the same evangelical beliefs except I would allow myself to be gay. If I did that, surely everyone would have to accept me. I could prove everyone wrong.

I was determined not to have sex until I was married, but I worried about that commitment. After all, since gay people were so super sex crazed, was I going to be able to find someone that would be willing to wait to have sex? Would my decision to remain pure mean that I would be eternally alone? Or would I have to compromise my values in order to find companionship? If I was thinking about compromising my values, did that mean I was already going back on my word? I was so scared, my mind spinning round and round and round with these thoughts. I didn't know who to talk to. I didn't know any other gay Christians personally and certainly none that were evangelicals. I felt alone, but I was determined to hold on to my faith and make peace with my sexuality.

When I started dating a woman and fell in love and she was willing to wait, I felt like I had hit the evangelical jackpot! This was perfect! I could do everything I set out to do! We would be chaste and do everything right. We wouldn't have sex until we were married. We wouldn't move in together until after the wedding. I could live out what all of my evangelical friends were doing just, you know, while being gay. It was totally going to work.

A couple months into our relationship, shortly after I came out, after I got home from a night spent at my girlfriend's house, my mom cornered me. Concerned. Was I being safe?

I was horrified! "Mom, I'm not having sex."

It was clear that she didn't believe me. She got this look on her face. "Well, I'm glad to hear that. But you have to understand how it looks. You stay over there a lot. You get home late."

"That doesn't mean I'm having sex," I responded.

She walked away. It was clear she thought I was lying, yet one of the things I was committed to was not lying to my mom. I wanted our relationship to be based on the truth. Sure, I sometimes omitted things or I didn't give her all of the details, but I didn't lie outright. It was a promise I made to myself; I wasn't going to be ashamed of my life and my decisions because I wasn't doing anything that was cause for shame. Now here I was, telling the truth, and my truth was being rejected for the narrative my mom had already made up.

I was so hurt that she didn't believe me. I was working so hard to fit into this evangelical mold and people just assumed stuff about me anyway! As I reflected on that particular exchange, I began to wonder why, exactly, I was so concerned about not having sex if everyone thought I was having it anyway! Why was I working so hard to remain "pure," to not go "too far," to protect my virginity when everyone around me thought I was already having sex? Where was this compulsion to "remain pure" coming from? Was it really something that God wanted for me, or was it something I was doing in order to please other people? More than that, what did it say about how people approached my sexuality that they automatically thought I couldn't or wouldn't be a "moral" person now? I was frustrated and hurt, more deeply than I could articulate. My mom's disbelief felt like an assault on my character.

This was the beginning of my deconstruction of the purity culture ethics I had inherited. As I learned more about my own body and needs, I also delved deeply into theology from different Christian traditions and into learning about the history of LGBTQ+ movements. I began to realize the tension I was feeling was not unique to me, nor was it new. It was both a deeply Christian tension and a deeply queer tension.

Throughout the history of the LGBTQ+ movement, there have been those who protested while wearing suits and dresses. There have been those who say, "We're just like you other people, only gay/lesbian." They fight for access: to marriage, to the military, to the American dream of owning a house in the suburbs with a good job and kids of their own. Meanwhile, there are others in the movement who don't want to assimilate. Whose identity reminds them of how the systems that exist don't protect the most marginalized. They don't want access to the military; they want to fight against the military industrial complex. They want protections, but not at the expense of more people being thrown into prison. There is a conflict between those who say that "respectability" is the way to get things done and those who say that being a part of the system is a problem.

This tension was present in the early Jesus movement as well; those who wanted to pay their taxes and stay under the radar of the Roman empire came into conflict with those whose belief in Jesus called them to stand against the empire in all its forms.

It seems the conflict resides in whether or not it's possible to change systems from the inside or if change only happens by creating something new. This call to either conform or rebel is complex.

From my experience, I learned that respectability would not save me. Being the "right kind" of gay was impossible because any single hint of depravity was enough to corrupt your entire being. In the black and white world of conservative evangelical thinking, a "good gay" was impossible. Either you were pure or you were corrupted. Either you were heterosexual or you were sinful. There were no degrees, no spectrums, no wiggle room. I didn't know that yet in my first relationship with a woman, so I thought I could contort myself into some semblance of acceptance. I could somehow still win people over. If I just did everything they wanted (only as a gay person) I could still have access to the heavenly club.

My mother's disbelief in my purity was a blow. It was another moment where I started to question how and if the beliefs I was holding on to were serving me. What good was my virginity doing, especially if it wasn't serving as a public witness because no one believed me anyway? Was there a point to continuing not to have sex? It felt scandalous to even consider the thought. Was this an idea I could let go of? And if so, what would that mean for me? Why was I holding on to this idea of not having sex until marriage? Was it possible to formulate my own ethics around sex and sexuality apart from those of the conservative church I grew up in? If I went down this road, what else would I be letting go of?

There is a pervasive idea that if you don't hold fast to evangelical sexual ethics (which basically boil down to no sexual activity at all until you are heterosexually married), then surely you must think anything goes. The slippery slope argument says that once you let go of the evangelical sexual ideal, then anything is up for grabs. There is no difference between sex before marriage and sexual assault on the sin continuum. It's all just as evil. Not only that, but allowing someone to experience pleasure might somehow unleash a sexual beast that will rampage without control. This is a deeply upsetting idea. The idea that reserving sex for heterosexual marriage is the only thing keeping people from rape and assault, from sexual violence, and from hurtful sexual actions says a lot more about how people understand and view sex and consent than it does about the morality of people who aren't evangelicals. And yet this ideal has permeated much of American culture, from abstinence-only sex education being offered in public schools, to the shaming of people in the media who are open about having multiple sexual partners before marriage, to the conflation of sexual violence with a lapse in moral ethics.

How did we get so out of tune? Is there another way to think about sex and sexuality with fewer absolutes?

Thankfully, both the story of Rahab and the sexual ethics of queer and trans Christians can bring us into harmony if we have ears to listen.

ᐁᐅ

Let's start with the story of Rahab. It might seem like a strange place to start. Hers is a fairly short story that appears in Joshua 2.

The spies from Judah enter the city of Jericho to check it out. Their job is to report back to the army what they will face when they attempt to destroy the city. The story tells us that at nightfall these men find themselves in the inn owned by Rahab, a prostitute. Because of course the men would find themselves in a "house of ill repute." The story is sparse on details, which leaves a lot to the imagination. Did these men "just happen" to find themselves in an inn known for being a place where you could hire sex workers?

I'm fascinated by Rahab. She is, as far as we can tell from the text, an unmarried woman. She's a business owner. She doesn't work for the inn; she owns it. She's potentially a madam, managing the women who work as sex workers in her inn. She supports not only herself but her whole family with this money. The spies don't seem to make any judgment about her line of work;

they are more concerned that she belongs to a people who are their political enemies.

Rahab is smart. She's wily. I imagine that to be a single woman, a business owner, and the protector of her family in a time when women weren't allowed to do much of anything, she had to be well nigh brilliant. She's savvy. When these spies arrive, she clocks who they are and what they are there for. She knows something more will happen. So, when the soldiers come chasing the spies, she hides them and then later on helps them to escape. As she comes to their aid, she also makes a deal: she'll help, but only if her entire family is spared when Jericho is conquered. She thinks like someone who is used to having to fight to get what she wants and needs. She knows how to use whatever power she has to protect herself and her family. She gets what she asks for.

The story of Rahab is just twenty-one verses in the larger narrative of Joshua winning military battles. She helps the Israelite spies escape. When they come back with the army to destroy the city, she follows their instructions (hanging a scarlet cord out of her window), and we presume she and her household are saved. We don't really know what happens to Rahab after this episode. We don't know if she was kept as a servant or slave. Was she allowed to live among them as a free woman? Did she keep her inn? Or leave it behind to travel with the Israelites?

What we do know is that Rahab ends up becoming a part of the lineage of Jesus. She is one of the five women mentioned in Matthew's genealogy (see Matt. 1:1–16, especially verse 5 for the mention of Rahab).

From sex worker to great-great-great-great-grandmother of Jesus.

Why does this story matter? Why was it included in the Bible?

There's something powerful and provocative about the inclusion of Rahab in the genealogy of Jesus. This woman was not a part of the Israelite community; she was an outsider, a foreigner. This woman would have carried sexual scandal with her. Even so, this woman somehow becomes grafted into Jesus's family tree. We are reminded that outsiders—those on the margins, those carrying sexual scandal—are part of the family of Jesus.

One wonders about Jesus growing up and hearing the stories of his family tree. We already know that his mother, Mary, was a fierce and uncompromising advocate for justice. She sings the Magnificat as a lullaby to Jesus still in the womb (Luke 1:46-55). She sings about kings being torn from their thrones and the rich being sent away hungry. She sings about the overthrowing of political systems. This is not your typical, quiet lullaby. Mary is a woman who carries in her a fierce flame for justice, a rage in her belly about the way things are, a deep sense that all is not as it should be.

As we read about the women in Jesus's genealogy, we are reminded of women who do what they need to do to survive. All five of the women mentioned carry some hint of sexual scandal: Rahab the sex worker; Ruth the foreigner who propositions Boaz in order to protect herself and her mother-in-law; Bathsheba, who is robbed of her name and was robbed of her husband and taken by King David; Tamar, who tricked her stepfather into doing the right thing; and now Mary, Jesus's mother, who becomes miraculously pregnant with the child who would grow up to change the world.

One wonders at how this impacted Jesus's view of the world. How it shaped the way he would later behave in his encounters with women. We sense in Jesus an occasional warring as he fights against patriarchal systems and the divisions of his culture. In one story, he calls a Greek woman a dog when she pleads for him to heal her daughter, but then when she claps back, he backs down and changes his mind (Mark 7:24-30). Then in another story, he has his longest recorded conversation in the Gospels with a Samaritan woman, an outsider who also has a hint of sexual scandal in her life (John 4:7–26). I wonder if she reminded him of the women from his lineage, if that's why he took so much time speaking with her. Then there was the woman caught in adultery (John 8:1–11), brought to Jesus by a mob who wanted to stone her. Even though it takes two to be adulterous, the man was nowhere to be found. Jesus not only defends her from her accusers but also sends her away without condemnation.

These outsiders were often the ones who challenged Jesus to expand his view even more. From the Greek woman who gets him to change his mind, to the Samaritan woman who gets him to talk about worshipping in spirit and truth, to the woman caught in adultery whom Jesus frees from an angry mob—each of these moments pushes Jesus toward the margins, both as he does his ministry but also in the way that people perceived him. Each time he made space for these scandalous women, we get the sense that he was taken as more of a threat by the religious and political authorities.

Sexual scandal has always been a threat to political power. From the way the early European colonizers murdered Indigenous two-spirit shamans and forced a Westernized heterosexuality on to Indigenous tribes that had long made space for more fluid expressions of gender and sexuality, to the mid-twentieth-century Communist scare in America that swept queer folks up in its net and used the threat of exposure to snuff out queer expression in film and the arts. We saw "homosexuals" in the thousands being swept up with other undesirables in the Shoah, an attempt to stamp them, us, out and eradicate our existence.[1] We see the ways societies continue to label queer and trans folks as the first threats to political order and power.

Sexual scandal also carries power: a sense that people are finding connection with one another outside of "approved" avenues. If you can find that connection outside of the "traditional" avenues then you are able to question other things, too. Suddenly, your questioning means you are a threat to the overall order of society. If you don't need the government to approve your life and your love, then maybe you don't need to buy into all of the other trappings either. Maybe you don't need marriage and the suburbs and the corporate job. And maybe if you talk about not needing those things, other people will see they don't need that kind of life either, and the whole enterprise of capitalism and power will fall apart. We can't have that, can we?

And so, questioners are pushed back into line. We are pushed back into our boxes. We are relegated to pursuing heterosexual monogamous marriage, life in the suburbs with the fence and the dog and the 2.5 kids, and the new car every year. The debt and the mortgage that keep us playing by the rules so that we won't lose everything.

The reverse of sexual scandal isn't morality or purity, you see: it's control. It's keeping us tied up into tight little boxes and punishing anyone who steps out of line.

When Jesus condemned divorce in the Gospels (see Matt. 5:31–32 and 19:3–9; Mark 10:2–12; and Luke 16:18), it wasn't about shaming people or trying to keep people trapped into loveless marriages; it was about protecting women. In that society, a man could divorce a woman for any reason at all. Divorce was easy and frequent, but the financial and social costs for women were astronomical. A divorced woman was left on her own, financially devastated. So when Jesus forbade divorce, he was in part trying to say to men who were being cavalier with the women in their care, "Stop doing that. You cannot leave someone defenseless. The kingdom of God cares about the most marginalized; you cannot claim to follow God and leave your wife homeless and without finances." And yet we've taken what was supposed to prompt caring for and protecting women and instead turned it into a prohibition of divorce that can lead to the very abuse Jesus was trying to prevent. When women are told they cannot leave their marriage for any reason, we put them in situations where abuse is excused. We put them in situations where they don't have a way out.

We tell queer people that if they act on their desires, they are depraved and outside of the will of God. We tell them that the way they are made is a test, and that the only way to follow God is to fall in line and sublimate what they long for. We shame them for who they are to make sure they stay in line.

ᐁᐁ

Even if we would never admit it, we often do rank sins, and somehow things that are considered sexual sins rank at the top of the list. Whether it's the way we've been impacted by purity culture or the control that patriarchal society wants to have over women, or the way that shaming people works to keep them in line, we approach sexual sin as the worst of all.

And yet in doing so, we excuse violence. We excuse those who abuse their power. We excuse those who hoard wealth and don't care for the poor. We excuse all manner of bad behavior—sin—that does deep harm to the world. Why? Why are we so fixated on naked bodies? On pleasure?

Why do we disparage sex workers who are trying to put food on their tables and care for themselves? Why do we shame the teenager who becomes pregnant? Why do we punish the consenting adults who happen to be of the same gender? We equate morality with chastity, and it hurts all of us.

We name things scandalous that really aren't. Scandal, to me, is something that violates the boundaries that keep the most vulnerable safe. Scandal is when a priest abuses his power and assaults someone. Scandal is when adults prey on children. Scandal is when a politician who wants to outlaw same gender marriage on "moral grounds" has multiple affairs with junior staffers. Scandal is about power and the abuse of it. It's not about adults who consent to be with one another. It's not about queer and trans people being honest about their identities. Being with my wife wasn't scandalous. Transitioning to male wasn't scandalous.

And yet, being branded a sexual outsider does impact how I move through the world. Being considered a gender outlaw impacts how I see society. I am grateful for my outsider status because it has required me to take ownership of my body and my ethics. The queer and trans people I find myself in community with have learned to think deeply about their sexual ethics. Being branded outsiders means they take nothing for granted. The ideas about sexual values handed to us can't be accepted without question. We can't take things at face value. We deeply explore and investigate and because of that, the ethics we hold are ethics that have been deeply considered. When we choose to do something, or not do something, it's because we have explored our options extensively and chosen what it most healthy. We do this by taking into account religious teachings, certainly, but also community obligations, the extent of our care for one another, and the world that we're trying to build together. Our ethics grow with us and are not limited to a bunch of boxes to check off.

Following all the rules doesn't make you ethical. I know people who waited to have sex until heterosexual marriage who treat their partners with disrespect. I know others who don't know how to handle the shame and trauma from their upbringing and so they ignore it and act out by being dishonest and cheating on their partners. I know some who use their virginity like a weapon to shame others.

We all know the stories of people who go to church every Sunday and who have spouses and children, yet have affairs. Is this behavior ethical? Is this behavior holy?

I'll push this idea even further. I also know polyamorous Christians who welcome every partner as if they were Christ. Who prioritize hospitality, communication, consent, and respect. They talk deeply and openly with people about desire, about shame, and about trauma. They hold space for one another and honor each other's needs. Are they unethical? Unholy?

Our notions about who is good and who is bad, our ideas about one size fits all ethics, our judgments of people who are different from us are not new. They are also not helpful. They create rigid categories that wound.

Maybe the sexual outlaws have something to teach us. Maybe there is something to be learned from people we consider touched by sexual "scandal" (when that scandal isn't coming from an abuse of power).

Maybe those who have lived and loved undercover can teach us something vital about desire, about commitment, about consent, about care for each other. Maybe those who have been pushed to the edges can teach us something about what it means to survive and even thrive.

Even those of us who are in monogamous marriages, who choose celibacy, or who are heterosexual have something to learn from those touched by sexual scandal. So many queer and trans folks through the ages have said yes to love and desire, have said yes to their knowledge of their bodies, have said yes to their truth, knowing it might cost them their families of origin, their place in the church, and even their livelihoods or lives. They said yes because they trusted that there was something powerful in that yes and it was worth the cost.

ᴖᴖ

Rahab did what she needed to do to make sure her family could survive. She became the protector of and provider for her extended clan. Not only is she not punished for this; she becomes part of the lineage of Jesus.

Mary, the mother of Jesus, also endured sexual scandal in order to say yes to God. She knew how she would be perceived. She knew what that yes might cost her: her future marriage, her protection in the world, and her family, and she said yes anyway.

We see it in the encounters between Jesus and sexual outsiders in the Gospels that challenged his thinking and in turn caused him to challenge the thinking of others by centering the most vulnerable.

Sexual outsiders have so much to teach us. Are we willing to listen?

CHAPTER 5

Ezekiel and Dry Bones: Healing Bodies

was ready to run out the door for a summer day of playing with my best friend, Chris. From sunup to sundown we ran wild through our wooded neighborhood, riding bikes, playing baseball, roaming the woods, and jumping over the creek. It was a taste of freedom, of fun. On this day, I was dressed and ready to go. Chris was already waiting, and I was impatient to get out the door. My mom called me into the kitchen.

"What?" I was exasperated.

"You need to put a bra on before you go play."

I could feel my face turn red. I didn't want to, but my mom was insistent.

I didn't want Chris to know what I'd been asked to do, so I ran back into my room and changed my entire outfit, putting on the bra as well. I felt uncomfortable and upset, but I shoved it down and headed out the door.

Chris and I played all day like we usually did. In the afternoon we headed into his kitchen for a snack. I loved snacking at his house because his mom bought the brand-name snacks my family could never afford. We ate Fruit by the Foot and drank some juice. His younger sister was hanging around and noticed my bra strap.

"Shannon is wearing a bra!" she announced gleefully.

It was such an innocent younger sibling thing to do, but I freaked out. Without even realizing what I was doing, I screamed at her: "Mind your own business! Don't talk about it!" She was laughing and Chris's mom told me to calm down, but I couldn't. I felt completely humiliated.

The emotions that were coursing through my body were alien to me. I could not explain them. I didn't know why they were so strong. I didn't know why this innocent teasing summoned such a rage in me. What I did know is my body was changing and I hated it, although I didn't have words for why I felt so uncomfortable.

Later that summer I was at my relative's house, wearing a bathing suit and swimming in their outdoor pool. Somehow the conversation came around to my growing chest. I was embarrassed again. My mom said to my aunt, "She'll appreciate those someday."

I jumped into the pool and submerged myself under the water so I didn't have to reply, but I thought, "No. No I won't."

As my body developed, I started wearing baggier and baggier clothing. My height maxed out around five feet five inches, and in high school I weighed about 120 pounds. I could easily have worn medium t-shirts, but instead I bought large and extra-large. The billowy shirts hung off my thin frame, but that's how I liked them. I wore baggy jeans and loose corduroy pants. Anything that felt even slightly tight got tucked into the back of my closet and never worn again.

I ignored my body as much as I could. I gave myself a litany of reasons as to why this was the right way to be. I told myself it was because I was so modest. I didn't want anyone to pay attention to me or my body. I was trying to be respectful of other people. But really, I was hiding. I didn't want anyone to see my body. I didn't want anyone to pay attention to how it was growing and changing.

I didn't even want it to be growing and changing. I felt strange and out of place when I had to wear dresses and skirts, and I finally started to win the battle with my mother for me to mostly wear pants, even to church.

I was comforted when I read words from Paul's letter to the Galatians that say, "So I say, walk by the Spirit, and you will not gratify the desires of the flesh. For the flesh desires what is contrary to the Spirit, and the Spirit what is contrary to the flesh. They are in conflict with each other, so that you are not to do whatever you want" (5:16–17 NIV). Or when I read Romans 8:6, "The mind governed by the flesh is death, but the mind governed by the Spirit is life and peace," I would think, "See? I'm just following what the Bible says. I'm paying attention to my spirit. I'm honoring the part of me that really matters. It feels good to have a spiritual reason to not want to be in my body."

But theology and bodies kept colliding. I was terrified the Rapture would happen, in part because I was taught that when we were "caught up in the air" we would leave behind everything that was earthly. We'd be taken up to heaven naked! I was horrified at the idea. What if I was on my period? What if people saw my naked body? Better to try not to think about it and pray extra hard the Rapture would wait awhile. Maybe when I got older, I would feel a little better about my body and not mind the idea so much.

As I entered into junior high and high school and the conversations turned more and more often to purity and modesty, I prided myself on how modest I was. I listened to the conversations my friends had about boys and I gave thanks I had virtually no interest in them. My lack of feelings about boys must have meant that I was pure, right? I was doing things right. I was a good Christian, a good girl. I would be okay—I repeated this over and over trying to convince myself.

Every February we heard a series of talks in both Sunday school and youth group about dating. Our leaders seemed out of their depth, unable to communicate with teenagers who were uncomfortable and giggly. I'm sure the other teens were getting at least some information from sex education classes in school, but as I was being homeschooled, there were large gaps in my information and knowledge. My mom was a junior high youth group leader while I was in junior high. I don't remember much of the conversations we had, but they all seemed to boil down to two main ideas: "If you are asking how far is too far, you've probably already gone too far." And "Don't have sex." As a bonus, we received an occasional aside about how bad abortion is.

> On the car ride home from one of these Sunday school lessons, my mom says to me, "I know you're not getting sex ed in school. Was there anything in that conversation you didn't understand today?"
>
> I shake my head no.
>
> "Did you understand the conversation about oral sex?"
>
> "Of course," I answer. "It's when you talk dirty to someone on the phone."
>
> My mother, to her credit, does not laugh at me. She simply explains what oral sex actually is, in overly clinical terms. I'm horrified. Why would anyone want to do that? It sounds disgusting. I can't imagine a world in which that would be something desirable. Once again, I give thanks for my modesty, trusting it makes me a good Christian.

My fantasies as a teenager weren't about sex; they were about intimacy. I didn't long to get naked with someone, but I did dream about having a close female friend I could set up house with. Maybe we would raise a kid together. (Part of my fantasy revolved around a girl "sinning" with a boy and getting pregnant, and then getting saved and needing help with the baby from a Christian, which, of course, I would be there to provide, along with a shoulder to cry on.) We would watch movies and be tender with one another. We would hug and hold hands. These weren't romantic feelings, I kept telling myself; I just wanted a really close friend. I had no idea that I was longing for a relationship. I couldn't wrap my mind around such a thing. I didn't know there was a name for what I was feeling. I had no idea other people were longing for the same thing.

All of this feels abstract, though, because I don't have access to my body. I don't feel like I know what my body needs and wants. I feel separate from my body as puberty continues to make it stranger and stranger to me. I don't want to think about my body and sex with boys, so I cut myself off from thinking about skin and flesh altogether. My fantasies are abstractions I can fall into without needing to name the feelings. Since I am so shut off from understanding my body, I don't know that the feelings I feel in my body when I dream about this hypothetical future with this nameless woman and "our" baby are romantic desires. When I think about intimacy, I am desiring romance. But since I have no sufficient language for my desires, I believe they are chaste and rooted in friendship, not romance.

And yet there are indications that other people don't see the way I am living with quite the same innocence that I do. In high school, I have female friends I cuddle with. We throw our arms around one another, or lean reclined into each other as we watch movies. Occasionally someone reaches out a hand and that hand is held. I'm not always the initiator, which helps me to feel that everything we are doing is "normal." All high school girls do this stuff, right? I just want to be affectionate with my friends. I want us to be close to one another. I really don't have any expectations of these friends other than friendship, and yet, looking back, I can see that adults in my life thought I was the aggressor pursuing more than friendship. The predator. It didn't matter if the other girls reached out for me first; it was my fault.

"You know, it's not normal for friends to cuddle like that," my mom
tells me after one of these evenings.
I balk, "We're friends. We want to be affectionate with each other!"
My mom is not convinced. I don't know what to make of her com-
ments. I feel ashamed but I don't know why. I just wanted to cuddle with
my friend; why was she getting so bent out of shape?

As each year of high school passed, I began to realize that my touch of girls was suspect. I began to wall myself off. I would long for a hug but refuse to reach out. I had been taught that my physical affection was a problem. It made me a threat. I held myself back. I made sure to hold myself apart.

The leaders present for my religious upbringing mostly talked about bodies in the negative. Our flesh was sinful. Our bodies were weak and frail. Our bodies held original sin. Our bodies would die and decay. The message, driven home over and over again, was that our physical bodies didn't matter. Our souls, on the other hand, were precious. Our souls could be saved. Our souls could be purified. Our souls were eternal.

That theological emphasis worked for me because I hated my body, so it was easy to focus on my soul and on being pure by ignoring my body. It was easy to focus on all of the stuff that was inside of me and pretend that this body didn't exist.

Almost everything in our faith conversations centered around what would happen when we died. People who were saved would go to heaven and be with Jesus. People who weren't saved would go to hell and suffer for eternity. In heaven, you'd have a perfected spiritual body. Everything that you hated about your physical body or was wrong with your body on earth would be corrected. I didn't know what happened to your body in hell; I guess it didn't really matter if it was fixed since it was just going to be suffering forever and ever.

Sure, we were expected to do good things on earth: we weren't supposed to lie or cheat or steal or curse. We were supposed to give 10 percent of all of our money to the church. We were supposed to pray and go to church and do our daily devotions. More than anything we were supposed to convert other people so they wouldn't have to go to hell. Beyond that, being a Christian mostly seemed like being a good person and hurrying up to get to heaven.

The idea of a Christianity that cared about bodies and what happened to them on earth was completely foreign to me growing up. I hadn't yet been exposed to any of the different strains of liberation theology. I didn't know about social justice work that was rooted in Christian faith. The verses about caring for the orphan and widow were mostly about giving them gift baskets at Christmas or supporting some kind of charity effort to make sure they heard about Jesus and got saved.

We talked about bodies only when we talked about opposing abortion and promoting purity. That was it. Otherwise, bodies were unimportant. Salvation was rooted in the spirit and soul. Our bodies were a side note. It made sense to ignore my body. It was easier. I could push it to the side and pretend I was holy because I wasn't focused on these worldly things.

But ignoring my body meant that I was cut off from who I was. Our bodies and souls aren't separate. It took an ancient vision from a Hebrew prophet to realize that I had gotten everything wrong.

ᴖᴗ

Do you remember the first messages you received about your body? Do you remember the first time you felt shame? Do you remember the moment when someone suddenly snapped at you, told you to stop touching yourself, or called you fat or chubby? Do you remember the first time you looked in the mirror and had a negative reaction? Where, instead of seeing yourself and loving yourself, you found a stranger staring back? Do you remember the way you examined every inch of your skin and criticized it? Was there a moment when you compared yourself to others and found yourself lacking? Where you felt like you weren't strong enough or muscular enough or handsome enough? Was there a moment when you were smaller than everyone else? Larger? Where you wished to be invisible so at least you wouldn't be judged? What did these experiences do to you? To your sense of self? To the way you carried your body through the room? To the way you clothed yourself? What did the church teach you about your body? What messages did you receive about the flesh and spirit divide?

We often talk about body image as if it's just something that affects people assumed to be female, but in every room I've been in and with people of all sorts of gender identities, when we are comfortable enough to be vulnerable, we discover we've all received negative messages about our bodies. Sometimes these messages come in the form of comments and other times because of actions done to us, but even if people didn't receive messages directly, they still absorbed them from the culture at large. It's hard to see defined abs and chiseled jawlines on every billboard and not have some thoughts about your own stomach and face. It feels like an almost universal experience to have discomfort in your body.

In my experience, the church hasn't been very helpful. Purity culture has been toxic and damaging within evangelical churches in particular, but even in churches without set modesty policies, the ways Christians have been taught to think about our bodies are harmful. Not to mention there are many churches that don't have space (literally) for different types of bodies. Older church buildings that don't have to apply ADA (Americans with Disabilities Act) standards (and claim they can't afford to upgrade to meet them). Churches without gender-neutral restrooms (for trans people, yes, but also for families and people with caretakers of a different gender). Sanctuaries with inadequate room for wheelchairs or with pews that are too small to fit a larger body with ease. Churches with steps up to the altar or an upstairs children's room with no elevator. All of these physical characteristics offer unspoken messages about what types of bodies are welcome in those spaces. Our buildings speak for us; they reveal who we were expecting, who we have made space for, who we want to be more involved. They also reveal the people who we haven't bothered to think about, who we haven't prioritized, who we didn't even think to welcome.

These messages are physical, yes, but at their root they are also theological. They give us clues as to what our church congregations believe about bodies. They reinforce the messages of culture that say only certain bodies are good bodies. We need to revolutionize our theology about bodies. Thankfully, Scripture has that revolution already recorded on its pages; we only have to do the work of shaking off centuries of harmful teaching in order to see it.

Let's start by dusting off the book of Ezekiel.

ᴑᴖ

In future chapters I'll tell more of the story of my high school and college years. In this chapter, to talk about bodies, we jump ahead to my time in seminary and when I started to understand my body more fully and how my reading of Scripture helped with that journey.

I started to really read the Bible in seminary. Oh sure, I knew Bible stories and passages before then, but knowing what's in the Bible and really understanding it are two entirely different things. Wrapped up in all of the things that I knew about the Bible were the very particular ways I had been taught to interpret those memorized verses. I hadn't been taught to read the Bible and notice. I hadn't been taught to read the Bible and ask questions. I had been taught to read the Bible so that I could explain Jesus to other people and make sure they got saved and didn't go to hell for eternity.

Ezekiel and Dry Bones: Healing Bodies

In a seminary class, I'm reading Ezekiel 37. This is the story of Ezekiel's vision of the valley of dry bones. Sometime earlier in my life, I had seen depictions of this passage in cheesy Christian art: Ezekiel raises up the bones and the vast field becomes a sea of dancing skeletons. Weird, creepy, kind of gruesome. Just the kind of strange Old Testament story I'd usually skip over. Now, I'm reading this passage with new eyes. Reading it, for the first time, to see what's actually there. Not what I've been taught. Not what I've heard others preach. Not what's in the weird Christian art on the internet. I'm reading to see what I see. What I find shocks me.

The book of Ezekiel takes place during a time when the people of Israel are in exile. They have been taken away from their homeland, their temple has been destroyed, they have been scattered and dispersed. As the years of their exile drag on, people die and are buried far away from their homes. The people who remain are starting to lose hope. They wonder if they'll ever get to go home again. Even more than that, for a people centered on homeland, they wonder what will become of all of the people who have died in exile. Will they be left behind? Will they be permanently separated from the larger community? What a sobering and scary thought.

The people are beginning to despair and Ezekiel, a prophet of hope, is trying to figure out what to tell them. In Ezekiel 37:1-14 (which I'll paraphrase below), the Spirit brings Ezekiel to this place. A vast valley. Acres and acres of land. Ezekiel looks, and in the valley is a sea of bones. Dry bones. Bones that have been there for a very long time. These people are dead. Like, *dead* dead. Picked clean. The Spirit tells Ezekiel that this is the whole house of Israel. (Thanks, Spirit! That's really uplifting! We're already losing hope and you bring me here and show me this? Not helping.) God then asks Ezekiel, "Can these bones live?" Ezekiel offers an enigmatic response along the lines of, "Oh Lord. You know." It's hard to tell if Ezekiel is being sincere or sarcastic, exasperated or honest.

God tells Ezekiel to speak to the bones. So he does, and there is a great rattling. Bone coming on to bone. That's what the artists grasp on to—that's where they usually stop, this vision of animated skeletons—but the story doesn't stop. The story keeps going: The bones come together, and then muscles and sinews lay over the bones, then skin on top of that. Bodies. Real, full bodies emerge out of this valley of super-dry bones.

Something is still missing, because Ezekiel is now looking at a vast field of full bodies, but they are still dead. *Dead* dead. God tells Ezekiel to call to the four winds. Ezekiel does. He calls to the winds and the winds come, the Spirit comes, and reanimates these bodies. They are now alive again. Standing on their feet. Breathing the breath of life. A vast throng, a crowd again: the whole house of Israel. Alive. No longer dead and far away from their homes; they are alive and present. No one left behind. Everyone accounted for.

This vision reveals the message Ezekiel is to bring to the people who are on the brink of despair. Your bodies matter. You are not forgotten. You will not be left to dry up in a strange land. This wasn't the promise of some home in heaven when you die. This wasn't a spiritual resurrection only. This was bodily.

In Ezekiel's vision these bones mattered. These bodies mattered. The sinew and muscle and flesh mattered. The breath of the Spirit that animated and gave life to these bodies mattered. It all mattered. What a message to receive!

I had never thought about my body mattering to God, not in this way. Not with this level of care. Earlier, I thought about my body's purity mattering to God and my body remaining unsullied by inappropriate touch, but this idea that resurrection might be bodily? The thought never really crossed my mind. While I had been worried about the Rapture, that happened to living bodies. The idea of bodies after death had always seemed fuzzy. We would get new, spiritual bodies, so it didn't seem like the body I was currently in was going to matter in the long term.

Now that I was reading the Bible with new eyes, all I could see was how bodies mattered. God didn't want us to remain in exile. For me the exile was within my own skin. I was living in exile from my body, even now. I had come out as gay in college, I had married my wife four years later and had sex, but I still spent most of my time hiding my body. I still couldn't make peace with my physical form. The realization occurred to me in that seminary classroom: if my body mattered, if my resurrection was going to be physical, if I was going to come back from exile, then I had some work to do.

The beginning of that work was to relearn what I thought I knew about the Bible and what it said about bodies. No more Platonic spirit and body divide. No more making excuses about the holiness of denying my flesh using the language of Paul. No, I had to understand myself as a whole person, body and spirit together.

Ezekiel's vision to give hope to the Israelites spoke to me through the ages and gave me hope as well. Hope that my body mattered, that I could make sense of this skin and bones, that I could return from my exile and find a home in my body again.

ᗡᗤ

What would change in our churches if we started to take the message of Ezekiel seriously? If we really, truly believed we, like Ezekiel, were called to bring the message of bodily hope to people who are feeling exiled?

This message of bodily hope isn't just for transgender people or folks who have been impacted by purity culture. This message isn't just about bodies and sex. This is a message about access to health care and medicine, access to fresh foods, access to safe and affordable homes. This is a message of freedom from police violence and brutality. It's a message of safety and peace that includes the whole person, body and soul.

When we think about our faith and our bodies in this way, we see the importance of food and nourishment. As much as I disliked the communion dinners of my childhood, I am grateful for the vision they cast of everyone coming to the table together. It's the same message Paul teaches in 1 Corinthians 11 (and even then, people weren't getting it right). He rails against the church in Corinth because some are leaving the meal hungry while others are getting drunk. He tells the people this meal is supposed to be an equalizer! All people should come to the table. All should be fully fed. Paul casts a vision of a community where all have enough sustenance, where bodies are cared for as well as souls. This is a vision we should be carrying into our churches today. A vision that takes as seriously the salvation of bodies as it does souls.

Neither a sole focus on salvation nor a focus on justice alone will be enough to offer the kind of transformation Ezekiel witnessed; we need a holistic approach. This is a both/and vision. A vision of spiritual depth and bodily wholeness. A vision of hope that encompasses all of who we are. A vision where no one is left behind in body or soul.

In Ezekiel 37:3, God essentially asks Ezekiel, "Will you speak to these bones and make them live?" In Isaiah 6:8, to another prophet, God says "Who will go for me?" These are questions that still resound for us today. What will we do to speak words of healing? What will we do to change belief systems that bring destruction? How will we respond to this question seriously as both individuals and as communities? We must bring a word of hope and proclaim with everything we do that yes, our bodies matter.

Jesus: In the Wilderness

My first real job was at a Perkins restaurant. I was hired as a host and worked through summer and school breaks starting in my senior year of high school. After my junior year of college, I was back at Perkins, waiting tables instead of hosting. Every day, I would get up and put on my black pants and white dress shirt and tie a necktie around my neck. I loved that uniform. I loved having a reason to wear a tie to work every day, even if it meant I got called "sir" a lot, which would then prompt my coworkers to tease me. I felt comfortable in those ties and that comfort gave me a sense of peace.

It's a normal lunch shift, waiting on several guests at once. I keep getting drawn back to one table, though, as I overhear snippets of their conversation. They are talking about church and youth ministry. After I give them the check, I work up my courage. "I heard you all talking about youth ministry. I'm in college studying to be a youth minister. What church are you from?" There was a pause, then one of the people answered, "New Britain Baptist. Hey, this is going to sound strange, but are you looking for a job?" I just stared for a moment. "Our youth pastor just left and we're looking for an interim who can keep things going for the summer." We exchanged phone numbers, and by the time they left, I had an interview just a couple of days away.

Chapter 6

I met with Pastor Tom and he hired me as their interim youth minister. I put in my notice at Perkins and took the job. From then on, anytime a bit of serendipity happened at New Britain Baptist Church (hereafter NBBC), we called it a "Perkins Moment."

Worshipping at NBBC marked my first time doing so regularly at a non-Grace Brethren church. It was hard to get used to at first. I didn't grow up with spoken creeds or scripted liturgy. I had never memorized the Lord's Prayer, so the first Sunday when I was asked to lead it, I tried to read it out of the Bible. Thankfully, the congregation knew it well enough to cover my stumbles. They were so gracious to me. They made space for my quirks and embraced my energy. But even in the immediate embrace, there were hints of struggle to come. Some people wanted me to dress differently or to not wear sneakers. Once again, how I looked was becoming an issue. I couldn't understand why it was such a big deal. I showed up on time, I showed up ready to go, and I was willing to step in wherever I was needed, yet it always seemed to come down to my shoes and my hair. To me it felt like a petty complaint—the thing people grabbed on to when they couldn't find anything else to complain about, but they wanted to put me in my place.

I shrugged off their comments as best I could and just kept showing up.

I worked at NBBC for the summer, falling in love with the congregation and the teenagers there, although I still had another year of college. I needed to head back to Indiana. Before I left for my senior year of college, I let NBBC know that if they were interested in holding the position for me, I was interested in taking it. I also told them that I understood if they needed to hire someone before I was done. I went back to college that fall figuring my time at New Britain was over.

Before I was even back on campus, I interviewed over the phone at a United Methodist Church a couple towns over from the college for an internship position. The interview questions were challenging to me as an evangelical. How would I respond to a kid whose parents were divorcing and came to me for advice? How would I confront someone about an issue in the workplace? I muddled through my answers as best I could and then was invited to attend an in-person service and interview once I was back in Indiana.

The First United Methodist Church of Goshen hired me as their intern. For the next nine months, I would drive thirty minutes each way on Wednesdays and Sundays to participate in the life of a church that was entirely new to me. I was in charge of the junior high program, bigger than any I had seen before. Sixty sixth- through eighth-graders were mine to lead every week and I was a senior in college. I was managing adult volunteers and though I, technically, would become an adult when I turned twenty-one in October of that year, I certainly didn't feel like one.

The First United Methodist Church of Goshen (hereafter FUMC) was a church in the middle of transition. A traditional, stone building stood in the middle of downtown. People there worshipped in wooden pews while singing traditional hymns. Outside of the town limits stood a new, multi-million-dollar family life center where people worshipped sitting in chairs while a band played on stage. The chairs on the floor were cleared away to turn the space into a basketball court. On Wednesday nights, hundreds of youth and volunteers would pack into that space, eat dinner, do homework, play sports, and then have their own time of worship and learning. This appealing programming drew kids away from FUMC on Sundays, too, when I'd be lucky to have two kids in my Sunday school class.

FUMC also helped me to understand that there was a world outside of the Grace Brethren Church. I had started to see that at NBBC, but FUMC brought it home in new ways. Their church had women who were pastors. They weren't openly affirming, but

Chapter 6

I got the sense that they were more accepting of the idea of LGB people than my college at least (which wasn't saying much, but at this point Christians who were even slightly more accepting were a revelation to me). I was able to ask more questions at FUMC. Teach more authentically. Lean in to theological curiosity.

There were days (weeks? months?) when I was a disaster. Overwhelmed with the workload of my senior year of college and ministry, overwhelmed with shifting ideas and identities, I know I wasn't always fully present. But FUMC became a safe place to wrestle a bit more externally. I was able to ask the pastor there about ministry questions I didn't know how to handle. I started to open up a bit.

On a Tuesday afternoon, just a few weeks into my tenure at FUMC, September 11, 2001, happened. I had just finished a fitness test for a class, come back to my apartment off campus, and collapsed onto my bed for a bit. I quickly showered and went to one of the many mandatory chapels. As I entered the room the energy felt different—off, somehow. Someone asked if I had seen the news. I hadn't. "A plane flew into the World Trade Center." I wasn't concerned. I made a joke about someone being drunk or tired and I didn't think much of it. I sat with some friends and someone opened the chapel with prayer. Then they said something about another plane. And the Pentagon. Now I was beginning to feel guilty about my earlier joke and wonder what was happening. Some people were visibly upset. We were praying, then another announcement broke in: a plane had gone down in western Pennsylvania. A lot of the students present were from that area. People ran out of the chapel to call their families. It was disorienting and upsetting. Classes were cancelled, so I went to a friend's on-campus apartment, where we watched the news and talked.

The next night at FUMC, I walked in to face sixty middle-school students who were terrified and afraid. The world as they knew it had come to an end and they were trying to make sense of things. I didn't have any answers. The youth group leaders and I mostly just let them cry and talk.

As Bryan, the associate pastor and my supervisor, and I walked to his truck that night I said, "I just keep thinking about those people who jumped from the buildings. The people who weren't saved. They jumped from one kind of fire right into hell." I was tortured by this thought, but at that time I absolutely believed that was what happened to anyone who wasn't a Christian. Bryan paused and took a moment, then simply said, "I'm not sure it works that way." I was floored. Of course it worked that way. That's what my church taught me from an early age. That's what I had always believed. That's what this entire Christian thing was built on: get saved and don't go to hell. What do you mean you're not sure it works that way? All of these thoughts raced through my head, but I didn't say anything. I felt a sense of self-righteousness at the time, but Bryan's statement stuck with me. It lodged into a crack in my heart and started to worm its way in. What if it didn't work that way? What then?

That was a question I would have to deal with later. I didn't have the bandwidth to handle the possibilities then. I was too busy trying to stay afloat. Running from class to theater rehearsals to class to church to rehearsal to home. In October of that same year, I received an email from New Britain Baptist Church. They had been in the midst of the search for a new youth pastor, interviewed people, and still hadn't found the right fit. Did I still want to be considered? I did. Could I come in for an interview when I was home on fall break? I could.

I went home for a whirlwind weekend of interviews: with the committee, with parents, with teens. I answered questions as honestly and clearly as I could. Then, I went back to college. I got the call from NBBC just a week later. They wanted to offer me the youth pastor position. They would hold it for me so I could start the summer after I graduated. I said yes, and then I had to explain to my mom that I was going to be a youth pastor. She wasn't so sure about it. I told her it was okay for me to be a female youth pastor because I would be under the leadership of a man. He was the real pastor; I was just the youth pastor. That's what I believed about women in ministry at the time, and that seemed to assuage her fears.

Life was golden. I had a job lined up for after graduation, I was in my senior year of college, and finally had a community of friends; I was making art and doing work I loved. Everything was rosy. I was even convinced, for about three months, that I could be straight. Or at least single. It was bliss . . . for a minute.

Then, the feelings I had for women started to come back. I had to finally grapple, seriously, with feelings that I had been trying to avoid for years. I could no longer completely avoid my sexual identity. I still didn't have sufficient language about gender, but even that fixed concept was starting to rattle around in my mind. Living off campus meant that I had freedom to do things like watch movies without getting permission first and even to watch things that were rated R! One night, I drove to Blockbuster and rented a film called *Boys Don't Cry.* It's the fictionalized story of Brandon Teena, a real person who lived in Nebraska. Brandon is thought to be a transgender man, living as a man and falling in love with a woman.

I watch the film, curled up on my couch, alone in my tiny apartment. I watch as Brandon talks about how he feels in his body. I watch as he falls in love. I watch as he is outed. I watch as he is brutally sexually assaulted, several times. I watch as he is murdered. I lie on my couch, frozen. Overwhelmed. Brandon was like me. Some part of my brain knows that there is something about him calling out to something in me.

I can't remember now if they use the word "transgender" in the film, but I just remember feeling such a sense of relief watching the story unfold on screen. There were other girls in the world who felt more like boys. Who wanted short hair and to wear baggy clothes. Who preferred the company of women to men. I wasn't a freak. I wasn't an outcast. I wasn't alone.

But then, the panic set in. I remember thinking: That's what happens to people like us. We are called names and considered fake. We are assaulted. We are killed.

It felt like there was no other future for me. There could be no other future for me. There was no hope. There was no triumph. There was only one ending to my story. I believed that because this was the only story I had ever seen myself in up to that point. I didn't know how to process the story or my response, so once again I shoved all of it down.

It kept coming back up. I could no longer ignore the feelings I felt for certain women that went beyond friendship. There was something else there. An attraction. A desire for physical intimacy (though I still didn't think much about sex—at that point I mostly wanted to hold hands and cuddle). I thought it was wrong and I prayed that it would go away, but no matter what I did or how hard I prayed, the feelings only seemed to get stronger.

What was God doing? I felt a silence from God I had never felt before. I didn't feel like I could talk to anyone about what I was wrestling with. If I came out as gay (or even struggling), I worried that I would get kicked out of college. My college had a strong lifestyle code for students and faculty, and homosexuality was definitely against the rules. If I told the pastor I worked for at FUMC or my future head pastor at NBBC, I worried that I would lose my jobs. I tried to look up some information online but I couldn't find much. I found some materials by SoulForce (an organization started by

Mel White to counter discrimination against LGBT people in the church) and read what they said about the "clobber passages" and how many people thought David and Jonathan were gay. It seemed like a nice thought but didn't impress me with its scholarly rigor. I sent an angsty email full of questions to their organization and got a very kind reply that I promptly filed away and never looked at again.

Yet I knew that I would have to make some decisions. Deal with this desire somehow. These feelings weren't going away. I decided I would be celibate for the rest of my life. I wouldn't tell anyone about my identity while I was at NBBC. They hadn't hired a gay pastor, so I needed to not be a gay pastor. Easy enough. I'd been pushing my identity down for years; I believed it would be easy to continue to do so.

I thought I had it all figured out. I told some close friends, ones who had mentioned other gay friends or acquiantances, that I was pretty sure I was gay, but I also reassured them that I would be celibate forever. At least that way I could talk to one or two people about the things I was feeling, the girls I had crushes on, and the way I was trying to wrestle these desires into submission. At least I had one or two people who didn't ask me about how I dressed or why I didn't date or talk about marriage. At least I had an oasis in the midst of what had been a desert of disconnection for years. Things weren't perfect, but they were better than they had been. Maybe that could be enough.

ᗣᗧ

My final years in college and the first few years after graduation were a bit of a wilderness. A wandering. I was set free from the mooring of the church I grew up in. I was being exposed to different Christian traditions and what I was finding called into question what I had grown up believing. At the same time, it felt like a balm to my soul, which had grown weary from constantly struggling with ideas and beliefs that didn't seem to fit anymore.

When I was doing this spiritual work after college graduation, terms like "deconstruction" or "exvangelical" weren't in the common lexicon. This was before Rachel Held Evans was writing about re-examining the concept of biblical womanhood and troubling passages in the Bible, before Matthew Vines went viral on YouTube with his experiences as a gay Christian. No one was talking about how to leave conservative evangelicalism but hang on to your faith. There were whispers, of course. The emergent church movement was getting started and leaders like Brian McLaren were writing books, but a lot of what was coming out of that movement felt like new clothing for the same religious ideas. The emergent church was either silent about or hostile to LGBTQ+ people. And for the most part, it was led by men. The movement of people was overwhelmingly white. I wasn't sure where I fit. I was still too evangelical to feel totally at home in mainline churches, but I was asking questions that were alienating me more and more from my evangelical friends.

I didn't have a road map. There were no memoirs of other people who had done this work. I didn't have access to any queer theology. The books I found about LGBTQ+ issues were really about LGB issues and mostly silent on trans people. Although I found some comfort in reading John McNeil's *The Church and the Homosexual* and Virginia Mollenkott and Letha Scanzoni's *Is the Homosexual My Neighbor?*, I didn't like John Shelby Spong's *Living in Sin? A Bishop Rethinks Human Sexuality* because he was too liberal and I wasn't ready for that kind of leap. I didn't have queer Christian friends. I didn't know anyone who had transitioned. I was alone with just the books I could get my hands on for a guide.

As a youth pastor who was only a couple years older than my oldest students, back living at home with a mother who was concerned about what college had done to her child, and feeling more and more alienated from the people I had grown up with, I struggled to make friends. I talked for hours on the phone with people from college and checked my email as often as possible, but for the most part, I spent my days alone. I would go in to the office to work, run youth group, then return home at night, and venture upstairs to my small apartment in the attic of my mom's house.

For the first time in my life, I had a steady paycheck, and I became immersed in pop culture as a way to keep the loneliness at bay. I would show up at the record store and DVD store every new release day and walk out with stacks of materials. On a road trip to visit a friend, I bought the first season of "Buffy the Vampire Slayer" on DVD and fell in love with this sarcastic, strong heroine and her group of close friends. I wanted my very own Scooby gang in real life, but for now, the ones on television would have to do. I fell in love with folk music: Indigo Girls, Ani DiFranco, Girlyman, and more. These media offerings started to give me two things I desperately needed: emotional catharsis and a sense of a larger queer community. I began to feel like I wasn't entirely alone in the world. Even if I still felt out of sorts as a Christian in the queer community, I at least didn't feel all by myself as a queer person.

As I came to terms with my sexuality, some things still rankled. I wasn't entirely comfortable with all of the feminine language of lesbianism. It didn't fit for me, at least not entirely. I still barely knew about transgender people and definitely didn't think I could be one. Trans people seemed even more out there than LGB folks. I was still trying to fit in a recognizable mold. To be the same evangelical I had always been, just gay. I wanted to be accepted.

I was desperately lonely. I no longer spoke with most of the people I had grown up with. Many of them hadn't gone away to college and they were still attending the same church. They still believed all of the same things we had believed as children and youth. It didn't feel like we had anything in common anymore. I still talked to my friends from college, but even in those friendships, cracks were beginning to appear. As I became more and more comfortable in my gay identity (even if I wasn't acting on it), those friends became more uncomfortable with me.

I was grateful for the few folks I did talk to regularly who accepted me, but phone calls weren't the same as getting to hang out in person. I went to concerts alone. I went to movies alone. I read books and watched TV alone. Occasionally, I would hang out with someone socially, but for the most part I was isolated. I didn't know how to make friends or find community. My mom kept pretty close tabs on me, so I was always worried about telling her where I was going and what I was doing. I didn't feel like I was allowed to stand up to her. I wasn't allowed to have my own life.

In evangelicalism, the children are always viewed as children, even when they are adults. And children are expected to obey every order, every request. Expected to acquiesce and offer respect. Standing up for myself was out of the question; it would have been seen as rebellion. I also worried about getting kicked out of my mom's house or having to move out. I didn't have a lot of money saved (and was pretty terrible about budgeting), so I had no financial safety net. I protected myself by playing nice, avoiding hard conversations, and keeping to myself.

My mother, of course, noticed. The more I pulled away the more she wanted to connect, but it seemed impossible to connect as we had when I was younger. My mother's faith allowed no questions or exploration. It was a faith designed to keep her safe and secure.

Questions from anyone, even her child, threatened that security. Our relationship was based on the same kind of unquestioning dynamic; our closeness was predicated on me believing, acting, and living the same way she did.

I was in the wilderness for those last years of college and until I started seminary, yes, but it wasn't a time of abandonment; it was a time of gestation. Something was being birthed. Something was awakening in me. First, I had to face my demons. First, I had to ask all of my secret questions. First, I had to examine my beliefs and weigh them and see what survived the refining fire. I needed to own my faith for myself. I couldn't simply accept what had been handed to me; I needed to interrogate it. My questions threatened the order of things and yet I couldn't stop asking them. The more questions I asked, the more my faith shifted and grew. I started to examine things I had always regarded as fact, things like the theological theory of penal substitutionary atonement. I had no idea there were faithful Christians who focused more on the resurrection than on Jesus's death. I didn't know the earliest Christians believed in the reconciliation of all things, not in a punitive God who would send some to hell. I could no longer take for granted what I had been taught, not what I once thought was the "gospel truth." I had to question all of it. It was the only way to make sure that my faith was mature, adult, and my own.

I don't think it's an accident we don't have a lot of stories about Jesus's life from when he was a child and a teenager. My sense is he was doing childhood and teenage things, figuring out how to walk and talk, figuring out how to read, maybe going to school and to the synagogue. Maybe he was listening to his mother sing protest songs, like the Magnificat, as she worked around the house, apprenticing with Joseph to learn carpentry. Through all of it he was developing an understanding of God and uncovering his relationship to God.

He would have grown up knowing his cousin John was a Nazarene. Kind of a weird guy, living out in the wilderness and eating weird food and dressing funny. (We all have that one relative, don't we?) In Luke 3:1–18, John's message about repentance is centered on justice. John tells those who come to him to share what they have with people who need it. He tells tax collectors to stop oppressing people by taking more than they should; he tells soldiers to stop harassing people. This word gets back to Herod, the ruler, and he isn't pleased. He blames John's arrest on John's critique of Herod's marriage to his brother's wife, but we can assume the radical nature of John's public ministry had something to do with it as well. Now, the author of the Gospel of Luke does a funny thing. In Luke 3:20 we are told Herod has put John in jail. In verses 21–22, we read about Jesus's baptism. The text is unclear about who baptized Jesus. It simply says, "When everyone was being baptized, Jesus also was baptized." We read there are voices from heaven and the Spirit descending. Then the author of Luke tells us that Jesus is around the age of thirty and gives us Jesus's supposed genealogy through Joseph.

I don't think it's an accident that the writer of Luke structured the story in this way. The author is saying that Jesus's decision to choose baptism, to choose this moment to enter public ministry, is tied to John's message and arrest. Jesus is choosing to take up John's mantle and carry it even further.

After the author's genealogical digression, we're back to Jesus, who is now filled with the Holy Spirit and led by that Spirit into the wilderness, where he is alone for forty days (Luke 4:1–14). We have a sense the Spirit knows Jesus needs time to integrate his new reality. He's had an incredible, life-shifting experience in the waters of baptism, and now he needs to figure out what it means for his life. Integrating a new reality is hard, and Jesus struggles.

He spends forty days alone. That's a long time to be on your own without human contact. No cell phone, no social media, no letters from home. Just Jesus and the desert. Alone. And fasting. You'd have to imagine that Jesus started confronting some pretty gnarly emotional stuff with that much time on his own. Every insecurity. Every doubt. Everything he had ever been afraid of. Every voice in his head, from every person he'd ever met, every time he faced someone telling him that he should just go back home. *Go back to Nazareth. Be a carpenter. Take care of your family. Don't bring more shame to your mother.* Then there were the other voices; the voice that came to him in the temple as a twelve-year-old that told him, "This is your father's house" (see Luke 2:49). The voice that came to him at his baptism and announced, "You are my beloved" (see Luke 3:22). This time in the wilderness will shape what's next for him. It will shape how he answers the call he received at his baptism.

After the forty days, when he is at his weakest, starving for food, possibly hallucinating, here enters his nemesis. Jesus's time in the wilderness is marked by his encounter with "the accuser." Some texts call this figure "the devil" or "Satan," but what strikes me about this series of conversations is that they could have been Jesus battling his own demons. His own fears, his own ego. We are, after all, often our own worst enemy. Sometimes the only person holding us back is us.

Jesus is first tempted to turn stones into bread. To someone who has fasted for forty days, this would have been an appealing thought. On the surface it seems pretty innocuous: just transform the stones. Eat the bread. No harm, no foul. But under the temptation something larger is at play: Will you use your power just to look after yourself? To serve your own needs? It's a question any leader has to grapple with: how will you wield the power you've been given? Good leaders know to use power to serve others, to make spaces more inclusive, to center the most marginalized. Jesus answers this first temptation to misuse his power saying, "People won't live only by bread." He's hearkening back to Deuteronomy 8:3 when people were recounting the story of Israel wandering in the wilderness. In Exodus 16 we read they were fed manna from heaven. Anyone who gathered more than their share found it infested with worms and stinking the next morning. Jesus knows the key to honoring God is for everyone to have enough. He passes the first test. He knows he cannot use his own power just for himself.

The next test is about safety. The tempter tells Jesus to throw himself off the mountain because angels will protect him. Again, there is something more complex happening underneath a suggestion for physical comfort. Will you sacrifice yourself only if you know that you won't actually get hurt? It's a huge question that will be relevant again when Jesus faces crucifixion. Does he only have the courage to face his path because he knows about resurrection? What if he doesn't know the outcome? What if he's not sure angels will really catch him? Or if God will resurrect him? What if he has to face the crucifixion and burial not knowing if he'll make it out alive? Will he still be willing to walk that road?

Finally, we see Jesus face the ultimate question. The accuser offers Jesus dominion over everything he can see. Sometimes when people read this passage picturing a literal, personified Satan, they focus most on this last temptation. Some claim the way this is phrased means Satan currently has dominion over the world and is offering that rulership to Jesus. Others say Satan is offering something that it isn't in his power to give, but I read this in a different way altogether, as Jesus deciding how he's going to be in the world.

He is being offered conventional political power. *You see all of this? You could rule over it. You could overthrow the government. You could take charge and set up a new government in its place. You could be a king.* He's being asked to consider political questions: What is the best way to make change? How do we change systems? He's also being asked personal questions: What kind of leader will you be? Is your power the most important thing? Can you set aside your ego to do what's best for the people? Will you serve instead of rule?

Who are you? Who are you going to be?

Jesus is the only one who can answer those questions for himself. He's the one who gets to decide what he's going to do when he walks out of that desert. We can imagine a world in which Jesus leaves the desert and starts a violent political uprising. A world where he aligns himself with the zealot movements that already exist, where he arms his followers, and they seek to overthrow the Roman government. We can imagine a world where he sets up a shadow government. We can imagine it because we've seen it over and over again in American political leaders, let alone in political leaders worldwide. We know what it's like to watch people strive for political or military power. We know what it's like to watch coups happen. We know what it's like to see armed people marching through the streets. Force and violence and power make sense to us because it's the world we live in.

Jesus makes a different choice. He looks at the political systems that were already in place and says, "I'm going to do something different. I'm going to be a different kind of leader. I'm going to hold up a different kind of vision of how the world could be. It's not going to look like kings and rulers sitting with their riches in their palaces. I'm going to lead with the least of these, with the shepherds and the fishermen and the tax collectors and the women. I'm going to lead with and for the outcasts and the rebels. The rejected and the ones bringing scandal." Jesus refuses to grasp for traditional political power. This is what the last temptation in the wilderness was all about, being an earthly ruler. Taking on the mantle of political power by any means necessary.

Throughout the temptations, Jesus relies on his religious tradition and upbringing to give him the courage to resist. He quotes Scripture not just in a duel of words, but because these Scriptures have been written on his heart. They are his source of strength and power. They bring him comfort and solace. These are not cheap words; they are the words of prophets and poets, of judges and holy people. Jesus repeats these words because he wants to be rooted in them. He wants to remain centered in his faith. He knows he'll need courage for the road ahead and that staying rooted will help him. Jesus was reminding himself of the core of his tradition: to focus on God as king, to center the community, and to imagine a different world.

He walks out of the desert having faced his temptations, having answered the questions for himself about who he is going to be. He returns from facing down his demons ready to enter into public ministry in a new way. He begins by going back to his hometown, entering his synagogue, and when it comes time for him to read, reading from Isaiah 61:1-2 (see Luke 4:16-20):

> "The Spirit of the Lord is upon me,
> because the Lord has anointed me.
> He has sent me to preach good news to the poor,
> to proclaim release to the prisoners
> and recovery of sight to the blind,
> to liberate the oppressed,
> and to proclaim the year of the Lord's favor."

And Jesus closes with, "Today this has been fulfilled in your hearing" (Luke 4:21).

This is a bold statement. Jesus declares himself in line with the prophetic tradition and right from the start, he tells anyone who would listen exactly what his ministry is about: the release of captives, healing for those in pain, the inclusion into community for anyone who had been excluded, and the year of Jubilee.

The year of Jubilee is an economic declaration of the cancellation of debts, the fallowing of the land, the release of slaves and servants. It was designed to be a giant reset button for a society that had drifted into injustice and economic unbalance. Jesus is saying, "We don't have to live like this. A better world is possible—one where everyone has enough to eat, where everyone has enough to live, where people aren't in service to the demands of others." But even more than that, Jesus is saying, "We can create this world that we long for. This world that God wants for us can be ours here and now."

It's this particular message of Jesus that is so frightening to the powers that be. It's a challenge to anyone in positions of power, anyone who has more than they need, anyone who relies on the subjugation of others to keep their state of living intact.

Jesus's time in the wilderness exposed the part of himself that he would have to continually face down. Dreams of power and control. Dreams of receiving official backing. Dreams of a way forward politically that would be easy and acceptable. He rejected those temptations and affirmed his commitment to be a man of the people, to center his life and ministry in and among the most vulnerable.

These kinds of questions are never answered once and then done. Throughout his ministry, Jesus would pull away from the crowds to check in with himself (Mark 1:35; John 6:15; and others). He needed to remind himself of who he was and what he was doing. He needed to continue to reject the temptations toward power and control. Jesus's time in the wilderness shaped his entire life and ministry. His continued pursuit of God and his calling was an ongoing process of becoming who he knew he was meant to be and was aided by the times he slipped off to be alone and pray.

Wilderness moments are vital for our maturation as humans and as followers of Jesus. My time in the wilderness was deeply challenging, and its reverberations are felt still today. My time in the wilderness makes me a better priest and writer; it makes me a better friend and partner. My time in the wilderness wrote the feeling of longing and loneliness deep into my bones. When I encounter people today who are lonely and longing, I have an empathy that is hard won.

My five years in the wilderness also taught me what it means to encounter God. A scary and overwhelming God. God away from all of the trappings of churches and community. An encounter where you are laid bare and forced to confront everything you thought you believed in. This encounter, like Jacob's wrestling match, often leaves you with a limp and also with a blessing. Without my time in the wilderness my faith would have remained shallow and secondhand. I would have held on to all of the things that I had been taught to believe in without true conviction. In the wilderness, I was pressed to determine what I really believed. What did I know of God? How had I encountered God in my life? What did my spiritual practice look like? No longer could those questions be answered by someone else or by reciting a memory verse or theological tenet. Those answers now needed to come from a place beyond words, a place beyond head knowledge—from the depths of my heart and soul. They needed to come from experience.

Throughout history, people have withdrawn from the community in order to have an encounter with the Divine. The ancient monastics who lived in caves and in the desert fled their lives in the city because they felt they couldn't find God amidst all of the hustle and bustle. As they fled, though, people always followed.

The followers wanted to know what the mystics had found and so the cycle of pulling away and re-engaging continues.

We wander in the wilderness to figure out who we are and then we bring our new understandings back with us. We share what we have learned during our wanderings. We come to terms with our psyches and the pain that hides in them. We confront our temptations and make decisions about who we are going to be. Then we come back into community, often challenging the places we once belonged to, to see us in a new way. When we re-engage, the question seems to be, Will the community be able to hold us once again? Will the community change with us? Or will our new understandings result in a fracturing of old bonds?

It's striking to me that when Jesus needed to decide what his ministry was going to look like, how he was going to change the world, he didn't go to the institutions to ask. He didn't go to his rabbi and ask for instructions. He didn't go to the synagogue or his parents. He didn't even go to his friends. He went to the wilderness. He needed to get away from what he knew. He needed to get away from the noise of other people's opinions. He needed to get away from the structures that held him in place. Jesus knew that the truth wasn't out there somewhere; it was inside of him. He didn't need more information, he needed to get quiet and to tap into the Spirit inside. He needed to hear the voice of God, and he could only do that in silence.

So often we believe (or are taught) that the answers to our questions are out there somewhere. Our parents have the answers, or the government. Our churches have the answers. We just need to do the right things: go to the right schools, get the right papers, get our diplomas and our credentials, and then we'll know what to do. Go to church and youth group, pray the right prayers in the right way. Follow the rules and we'll find the answers.

Yet over and over again in the Gospels, we see that Jesus goes off by himself and seeks quiet. When he feels pulled in a certain direction, rushed or pushed, he finds somewhere to be alone and he gets centered and knows what to do next. Over and over he turns inward. He seeks God in prayer, he listens to his own deep knowing, and that's what points the way.

Transgender people know something about being in the wilderness. Many of us have lived most of our lives in it. Transgender people know something about needing answers. And often we're told that we can't know or trust our own bodies. We're sick, we need therapy, we definitely shouldn't medically change our bodies. But when we get quiet, when we are alone, when we can clear away all of the noise and opinions and hate speech, we know that there is something we need to do in order to uncover who we are. When we get quiet and get in touch with our bodies, we know the truth of who we are, no matter what anyone else says. And throughout our transitions, we keep having to return to that quiet place and getting back into touch with our center being, and every time we hear, "This is who you are. Do what you need to do and be at peace." We jump through whatever hoops we have to jump through, we tell our stories over and over again, we insist that we know who we are and what we need. The confidence to do that doesn't come from studies or reports or medical journals; it comes from the quiet inside of us that we can only find when we go deep.

Where was your wilderness? Was it a place? A period of your life? A moment in time? What did you find out about yourself when you were there?

All of us, not just queer and trans folks, have experiences of wilderness, those times when we are separated from everything we thought we knew and forced to confront the deepest parts of ourselves. Some of us are totally freaked out by this prospect and run from the wilderness back into our old life before we find answers. We fill our days with activities and meetings. We dull our feelings with substances, with endless scrolling on our devices, or with relationships. We throw ourselves into serving our church or our family as a way to avoid the questions in our minds. We do whatever we can to run from what we fear the wilderness will show us.

Others of us lean into the wilderness. We don't flee it; we embrace it. We go deeply into the inner recesses of our lives to find out what's there. We wrestle with the questions, the fears, the doubts, the contradictions. We confront the things in our hearts that disappoint us—our pettiness or jealousy, our anger, our addictions, our failings. We become still, we clear our minds, and then when we are ready, we leave the wilderness and shed our old lives and make space for what's new.

The wilderness is terrifying. It's harrowing. To face it requires intention and care. It requires us to have the courage to stay in one quiet place for a bit, to listen to what the Spirit is telling us. It requires us to face up to the times we've failed and to plan to make amends for those times.

We can also get stuck in the wilderness. We can get stuck in the anger and self-loathing. We can get stuck in unhealthy cycles of thought or emotion. We can leave behind our old lives and beliefs but never build something new. Instead, we may simply sit in the wilderness, lost. We may wander for years, making this a leaching time instead of a generative time. For the wilderness to be a place of life and not death, we have to change our approach to it.

Maybe you're in the wilderness now. You're realizing that the things you were taught and the things you once believed wholeheartedly are no longer life giving. Maybe the church you've been a part of doesn't have space for you to ask your questions or for your new identity (or your child's/spouse's new identity).

Maybe you're realizing that you've done everything "right" and you're still not happy. You went to a good school and you got a good job, but something is missing. You married the person you thought you were meant to be with, but the spark is gone. You've devoted your life to the church, but you can't hear God anymore.

Or, maybe you're feeling like everything in your life is great but you could be doing more: more work for justice in the world, making more changes to live in line with your values. You feel like you could be connecting to God and others on a deeper level, but you're not sure how. You're feeling rattled, shaken, wondering what's next. You're looking around and wondering if you're going to lose everything on the other side of the wilderness.

Coming out of the wilderness and embarking on your unique calling and ministry requires a change in behavior. Your life changes. Change is scary. It's disorienting. It can cause fractures in relationships. It can make places that once felt like home now feel stifling and suffocating. So many of us do our best to avoid the work the wilderness requires. We stay where we are, even if where we are no longer fits, because it seems easier than moving toward what's next.

We hold on to identities and labels that no longer fit us: evangelical, straight, married, male/female, conservative, liberal, compliant. We may stay put, but once we've gotten the taste of something else, something more satisfying than we once had, all of the tastes that used to bring us comfort start to lose their flavor. Once we are confronted with a new future it's hard to unsee it. Even if we choose not to move toward it, we've had a glimpse, and that glimpse haunts our vision.

It's only in moving toward what we know to be next that we can leave the wilderness whole. By confronting who we truly are, we can make the changes necessary to be who we know we can be. It's only by getting clear on what's required of us that we can move toward the future we long for.

A whole lot of people get stuck in the wilderness. Or they flee from what they learned there and squander their calling in favor of the familiar. But the brave ones, the ones who do the soul work and come out of the wilderness ready to move: those are the ones who shift the world. Don't you want to be one of them? Will you do the work your time in the wilderness has revealed to you? Will you do the work the Divine is requiring of you? Will you answer the Spirit's call to be your unique and wild self in the world? Will you go even if it leads to a cross?

The Transfiguration: Truth Telling

I t will be National Coming Out Day soon. Share your coming out moment. Elliot Page came out. When did you come out?

The way we speak about coming out leads people to believe that coming out is a once and done experience. You come out and then you're out. It's not exactly like that.

Coming out is a process, both privately and publicly, and in some ways, you never stop coming out. There are new people entering your life who may or may not know your story. Even if you're married or out in a very public way, you may run into someone who doesn't know you, who assumes you have a husband when you actually have a wife, someone who assumes that you've always moved through the world as male, someone who assumes that every person is straight and cisgender. Each time, you make decisions in the moment: Does this person need to know who I am? Am I safe (physically and emotionally) to reveal myself? Is it worth whatever negative reaction this might evoke? Coming out is an ongoing experience.

My first inclinations that I might not be straight were in high school. I scribbled a note to a dear friend because I didn't have the courage to say it out loud. I told her about my "struggles with homosexuality" and I hoped that she wouldn't reject me or feel weird about our friendship. I couldn't say I thought I might be gay. If you said something like that then you were in dangerous territory spiritually, but if you "struggled with homosexuality" then there was still hope for you. Thankfully I wasn't rejected, at least not in that moment, and I felt a little lighter having someone to share the burden with. Even though I edged a toe out of the closet, the door was still mostly shut and would remain so for several more years.

Partway through college, I realized my struggle wasn't going away. No matter how hard I prayed or how many times I rededicated my life to Jesus, the feelings I was experiencing were still there. The most I could do was shove them down for a while, but they always came back to the surface.

At this point in my life and journey, I didn't have any examples of healthy queer Christians to look up to. I didn't know anyone who had managed to hang on to their faith and be themselves as well so I didn't think it was possible. I was destined to a lifetime of loneliness because I was gay. It felt like a cruel trick, like some kind of sick joke. God seemed capricious and nasty. To create me with feelings I couldn't control and God wouldn't take away and then expect me to deal not only with a hostile society but also a hostile church and religion? What was the point? What was God trying to do here? Was this a test? Or was God kind of mean? It seemed those were the only two options to ascribe to God with the understanding I had from what my church taught. If God was all knowing and all powerful, with a predetermined plan for each person's life, then everything that happened to us in life was part of that plan. This test, this trial, must have been part of God's plan.

The ambiguity of the space I was living in felt untenable. It felt like I had all of these walls surrounding me. No matter how close I was to someone they couldn't know all of me, not until they knew this truth. I was sick of hiding, sick of feeling separate from people.

I began to tell some friends in college I was gay but assured them I wasn't going to act on it. I would live a life of celibacy and singleness and maybe God would deign to love me; or, at the very least, maybe I could avoid hell.

In the beginning of my journey I considered that I would be truly out when my mother knew. She was my barometer. Everyone who knew up to that point in time didn't count as a total coming out experience because my mother was the final boss. When she knew, then I would be out. Probably not proud, but at least out. I wanted to make sure I was ready before I told her. Ready meant a lot of things: emotionally ready, scripturally ready, financially ready.

I wanted to make sure that when I told her, I would be able to handle it emotionally if things went badly. If she said things or did things that were hurtful, I needed to know it wasn't going to wreck me. I also wanted to make sure I would have answers to her inevitable questions. I felt like I would need to be able to defend myself using the Bible. I needed to know the meaning of every single "clobber passage" and I needed to be able to share those meanings calmly, clearly, without too much emotion (but definitely with some emotion or else she would think I had "hardened my heart"). I needed to be able to share every answer without stumbling over my words and be ready with those answers as soon as she asked.

Finally, I needed to be ready financially in case she kicked me out of her house. I wanted to make sure I had another place to live lined up, I had money in the bank, and my car was in working order. I didn't know what would happen when I came out to my mom, but being prepared felt necessary.

I waited. And waited some more. And then the decision about when to tell my mom was taken out of my hands.

This was the first in a series of outings: by a hospital visit, by a bumper sticker, and by a MySpace page.

I had been introduced to Amy by a friend who thought we might get along. We loved the same kind of music, and after years of going to concerts alone I was excited to have a friend to go with. We met the first time at a gig she was playing in New Jersey. After it was over, she introduced me to some other friends and we all went to a diner and hung out until the wee hours of the morning. More concerts and late-night conversations followed. I'd stay up talking with her until 4:00 a.m., get home, sleep for a couple of hours, and then go to work. This wasn't the plan, but we were falling fast for one another. Neither of us was ready for it. She was still recovering from the bad breakup of a long-term relationship; I was still living at home and working for a church where I wasn't out. The church didn't have a clear stance on LGBTQ+ issues; there was at least one openly gay member, but no one really talked about his sexuality. I wasn't sure how the majority of the congregation felt. I knew who the people opposed to affirming LGBTQ+ members were; they were loud and anxious, so I wasn't sure how much support there would be. I hadn't intended to date, at least not while I was working at the church, and yet here we were.

Amy was someone who was okay with my faith, who was honoring of my desire to wait until marriage to have sex, who was creative and funny and fun to be around. I felt like I had hit the jackpot, except for the whole church/mother/ministry thing.

As I fell more deeply into my feelings for her, my attention was all over the place. I was working full time at the church, trying to keep my new feelings a secret from my mom, and spending as much time as I could with Amy, who lived an hour away. We were in the heady stage of new love, the space where you drive home as the sun comes up and run on the fumes of emotion. Even in your early twenties, though, you can only keep up that kind of pace for so long.

I had the added pressure of not being able to talk to anyone about what I was experiencing. I didn't have friends I could share my good news with. I couldn't talk about my split attention at work because I had made a commitment to myself that I wasn't going to date. I definitely couldn't tell my mother that I was falling in love (though, in hindsight, my being away from home until all hours of the night probably wasn't the best way to keep a secret). As I fell more in love, I felt the stress of work and home building. I didn't know how to navigate these new waters because I never expected to be swimming in them. The few gay people I did know weren't part of conservative Christian families and churches. I had no one to talk to. The pressure built and built.

Sometimes, before I would go in to work, I would get hit with a wave of nausea. I couldn't control it and would end up throwing up. When I vomited, the nausea would go away and I could get on with my day. Weird, but not debilitating, so I figured it was probably fine. Then it started happening every day. Then it happened every time I ate. I went to the doctor, worried I had acid reflux or maybe even throat cancer (my grandfather had died just a couple years before of throat cancer and he became aware of it because of a simple cough he couldn't get rid of). The doctor examined me and asked, "Are you under a lot of stress?" I laughed. "Yes."

Yes. I'm a closeted Baptist youth pastor working in a church and living with my mother. Yes, I am under a lot of stress. I wanted to tell him everything. I didn't. He prescribed some medication and told me to schedule another appointment. I left feeling frustrated.

The nausea kept getting worse. The new medication helped a little bit, but not enough. Then it got really bad. I couldn't keep any food down at all. For several days I threw up everything that I ate. I had no energy. My mom came up into my attic apartment to find me lying on the floor. I just ran out of energy and laid down where I was.

She drove me to the hospital where they hooked me up to IVs and said that I was dehydrated, but that otherwise there was nothing wrong with me. Those were the days before texting was really a thing, so I called Amy after I was released from the hospital. Even though we were careful with our conversation because my mother was in the car, I'm sure there was something in the exchange that gave us away. Whether it was the tone of my voice, or my insistence that I needed to call her as soon as I left the building, I had the sense that my charade was about to end.

About a week later my mom and I were taking my little sister to the movies. She was in the back seat listening to some kind of Disney music on a CD with her princess headphones. I was excited to sit in a dark theater and watch something fun with my family. We were not too far from the theater when my mom said, "I saw Amy's bumper sticker."

Oh shit. I felt the fear overtake my entire body. I had been so worried about that damn bumper sticker. I had asked Amy to back in her vehicle whenever she was parked at the house, trying to hide the sticker. She thought it was stupid, but obliged. I guess we hadn't been careful enough. Amy belonged to a UU (Unitarian Universalist) congregation and had one of their stickers on her car that said, "Civil marriage is a civil right." (Those were the days when civil unions seemed like the best that the LGBTQ+ community could hope for.)

Time slowed down. I was aware of my breathing speeding up and my heart racing. I contemplated throwing myself from the moving car.

My mom continued: "Is Amy a homosexual?"

I answered, "Yes."

A brief moment of silence before she lobbed the next question. "And is that the nature of your relationship?"

There it was. The question I had been dreading. The answer I wasn't ready to give. I considered lying. I decided not to and simply said, "Yes."

Silence. My mom launched into a litany: "You know it's wrong. . . ." She compared me to my stepfather, who had had an affair. I just sat there unable to come up with a rebuttal. All I kept thinking was, "It's done. It's done. She knows. I'm out."

We got to the movie theater and went inside. I tried to text Amy but the reception was bad. I sat through *Madagascar* with my little sister bouncing in the seat beside me and wondering what the hell had just happened. My anxiety was through the roof, but I felt like I needed to keep up a good appearance for my sister. We all went to lunch afterwards and everyone pretended like everything was fine. I felt like my entire world had shifted on its axis and I didn't know what it meant for me. The moment that I had been planning for and dreading and worrying about had happened; now, it was done. What did that mean?

Just a month or two later, the church I was working at hired a new senior pastor, and I knew it was time for me to go. In my initial meeting with him I had asked about supporting gay kids in the youth group. His evasive answer made me know this church was no longer going to be a safe place for me to serve, but even more than that, I wasn't going to be able to make it a safe place for the youth I was called to serve either. It was time for me to resign. I told the church leadership I was planning to leave NBBC at the beginning of the summer. I would stay through the transition to the new pastor, but then I was going to move on to other things.

Two weeks before my final Sunday, I got a call that the new pastor and the head of the church council wanted to see me. I called someone I knew on the pastoral relations team and he couldn't give me a lot of information. I felt sick to my stomach.

I walked into the pastor's office, and on the desk I saw my MySpace page printed out. The profile photo was of me kissing my girlfriend. One of the youth had found it and told her parents, who then told the pastor. Everything I feared was coming to a head. I was told that since I was already resigning, they were going to let me finish out my time. I was supposed to preach on my final Sunday at the church, but the pastor said they weren't going to let me do that. "We don't want to set a bad example for the youth." I was furious but held my tongue. I didn't want to make things worse.

For four years I had served this church, and now it was all being disregarded because of the homophobia of the new minister. In reality I had done nothing wrong. What I did on my personal MySpace page was my own business. I wasn't dating someone from the church. I hadn't crossed any lines or boundaries—there were no official church rules about not being gay—so this response seemed simply punitive from someone who didn't like gay people.

On my last Sunday my girlfriend came with me to the church. One of the families, people who had been in the church for generations, pulled Amy to their side and told me, "She'll sit with us. And if anyone comes for her, they'll have to go through us." It gave me a sense of hope to know at least I had some allies there.

I thought after I came out to my mother and left the church that my coming out journey would be over, but there was one final round of coming out I needed to do. First to myself; then, again, to my mother.

In the year after I left NBBC, Amy and I continued to date and decided to go to Canada to get married (where it was legal). I worked odd restaurant jobs and tried to figure out what was next. I discerned that there was still work for me to do in the church, and so I applied to and was accepted into the Master of Divinity program at Union Theological Seminary. Amy and I got married two weeks before I started seminary. Throughout this time, I continued to struggle with how I felt in my body. "Lesbian" didn't entirely fit as an identity. It felt like not enough. I tried on "genderqueer," but that, too, fell short. Then I started to read about transgender people and the pieces clicked into place. Finally, after all these years, I had language for my gender identity, and when I finally came to terms with it and was able to say the words, "I'm transgender," I knew I needed to transition and start living as myself. I was heading into my second year of seminary. The thought of coming out over and over and over again felt exhausting, so I composed an email.

Hello to all:

I will just take a brief moment of your time. I know a lot of you don't know me, but I just wanted to take a moment to share something with all of you:

It is after much soul-searching and introspection that I have realized that I am transgendered [sic] and will be looking into the possibility of transitioning from female to male. I will greatly appreciate your thoughts, prayers, and support as I embark on this journey. I am not changing my name, but I would ask that you begin to use masculine pronouns to refer to me.

I appreciate you taking the time to read this and hope that this new semester is going well for everyone.

Grace and peace,
Shay Kearns

And then I sent it to the entire student body, faculty, and staff. In hindsight it was maybe a bit too much, but it mostly did the trick. I received several messages of love and support and the word was out.

Even though people at the seminary now knew, they still struggled to get my pronouns right. I sometimes wonder if it would have been easier if I had changed my name as well, if the combination of a new name and new pronouns would have cemented it in people's heads more firmly, but I didn't change my name. For the next two years, I had to deal with being misgendered. Some folks eventually got it right; others refused to adjust even after a full year of my medical transition. It was disheartening, frustrating, and exhausting to feel like I needed to continually correct people.

I often felt anxiety on campus. Should I use the men's restroom? Should I go across campus to the library and use the gender-neutral restroom there? Will people use the right pronouns for me today? Will I have to correct someone in front of the whole class?

I was asked to consult about seminary housing policies (even though I didn't live on campus). I had to endure a transphobic professor in one of my classes. I felt like I was a walking "Transgender 101" workshop. At any and every moment, I needed to be prepared to educate people about my identity (an identity I had only recently begun to be able to name) and my entire community (a community I was still just getting to know).

I was also spiritually fragile. Seminary was a time of much-needed deconstruction of the remainder of the theology from my evangelical childhood. I was learning to read and study the Bible in entirely new ways. I was learning about the history of the church, but even more importantly, the history of various doctrines that I had been taught to simply accept and never to question. Learning that many of the things I had been taught were handed down from Jesus were actually much later inventions produced hope and felt staggering. My entire foundation was being taken apart and rebuilt. Theology had become an academic endeavor.

The intellectual nature of Union was a balm to my weary soul. After years of struggle to come to terms with my identity, of believing that God was going to hate me, of fearing that I would lose my family and friends and even my very soul, to be able to hold my faith at arm's length and study it for a while was a relief. I could set aside notions of needing to have all of my theology and faith exactly right and instead look at things from all sides. I could gather ideas and hold them up to the light and see which ones shimmered. I was able to stop seeing every single belief as a potential ticket to hell forever.

This intellectual nature had repercussions, though. My faith had been emotional and heart-centered when I was growing up. My church talked about faith in terms of relationships and love. The Bible was called "God's love letter." From the singing of worship songs with one's hands in the air, to the practice of reading daily devotions that were all about growing closer to a God who loved you deeply (one of the rare, less judgmental portrayals of God in my church), I was taught that faith was meant to be emotional. Now that my faith was more intellectual, I felt out of sorts. I could look at the theological environment I had grown up in and see how my emotions were often manipulated and how that manipulation was unhealthy for me. At the same time, I missed *feeling* like I was part of something bigger. I missed the emotional connection. I missed the heart.

I wasn't sure how to bring the head and the heart back together in my faith. I wasn't sure it was even possible. Before I could even attempt that reconciliation, I needed to figure out how to tell my mother that I was trans.

I didn't know how to tell my mother this additional news. Even though she had been remarkably more accepting about my first coming out than I expected, I didn't think this one would go over as well. I grew up hearing stories about how when she was pregnant with me, she just knew she was going to have a daughter. How she only picked out one name. She seemed so invested in my feminin- ity. From the dresses she forced me to wear in childhood to the way she grieved over my short hair, I felt telling her I was a man would be a bridge too far. I worried she would forbid me from seeing my siblings and that she would cut me out of her life entirely.

I also felt like I just barely had the language to explain my gender to myself, but even that language was going to be too complex to communicate with my mom. I was just now learning that transgender people existed, so what did she know about them? How could I explain it to her in a way that she could understand but felt true to my own experience? I had no idea.

So, I didn't tell her. I came out to my classmates in September, I started taking testosterone in January, and still I didn't tell my mom that I was trans. I didn't know how. I knew I needed to, but I wasn't sure what to say. As I was beginning my journey toward being openly queer and dating someone, I felt like I had to have every hard conversation with her face to face. I felt I owed her that for making her life hard. Even though I hated those face-to-face conversations, even though I left them feeling like I hadn't said what I had really wanted to say or explained myself very well, I still felt obligated.

After months of agonizing, I decided that this time I was going to come out on my own terms instead of being forced to respond to questions. I was going to write her a letter. A letter would give me the time to think, to reflect, to choose my words carefully, to be measured and calm, and to express myself in the way that felt most comfortable to me. But first I had to write the letter. And decide when to send it.

I told myself I had time. The testosterone would take a while to work (more to come on this process in chapter 9). It would be months until the changes were really noticeable. Several months into treatment, I called my mom on the phone. She asked about my lower voice. "I think I'm getting a cold," I covered.

A month or two later, my little sister picked up the phone when I called. She didn't recognize my voice. I knew the time had come to explain what was happening, but I still didn't feel ready. I stopped calling home for a while. I avoided my mom's calls. Finally, I decided that I needed to send this letter. I couldn't wait any longer. I went to the cafe at the Borders bookstore near my house and told myself I couldn't leave until the letter was complete. I wrote it and rewrote it trying to find the right words: the words that would somehow allow my mom to hear me, the words that would break through her religious walls to allow her to see her son. I finished the letter. That very afternoon I went out and dropped it in the big blue mailbox on the corner, a place where once I released the letter I had to let it go. There was no going back.

I waited for the response, stressed, anxious, but glad it was finally out there. Several days later I got an email from my mom. She wrote, "I need time. But I love you." That was better than I was expecting. At least she said she still loved me. Maybe we would get through this!

A longer email followed, leaving me more hopeful still. Then, on my twenty-eighth birthday, I received a phone message that was accusatory and insinuated that my mom didn't want my sister to talk to me or see me. I was crushed.

It went on like that, a couple steps forward, some giant steps back, finally settling into a space of her mostly ignoring my transition. My mom occasionally made an effort to call me her kid instead of her daughter, but she refused to use the right pronouns for me. Even as I was unmistakably male. Even as I changed my identification cards and my birth certificate. Even as no one else on the planet called me "she," my mom wouldn't budge on this issue. Every time I heard "she/her" instead of "he/him," it felt like the prick of a knife. One prick won't kill you, but enough of them add up and you might just end up bleeding out. That's how I felt, like I was bleeding out, yet also that no one could see the blood but me.

Coming out isn't a one-time thing. It's a process. It's often painful, but more than anything it's exhausting. To put yourself on display, to tell your deepest truths, to hold them up, and then to allow other people to cast a judgment on them is tiring. It's not about telling your secrets; it's actually about revealing your truth. The problem with the way society has set up coming out is it allows other people the opportunity to decide whether or not they will accept your truth.

As recent years in American politics and global health crises have taught us, just because you refuse to accept an idea or a belief doesn't mean that it's not true. Yet we've set up a system where someone can refuse to acknowledge the truth and then fall back on, "Well, that's just what I believe," or, "My faith says I can't condone this." People use their faith to hide their bigotry.

Coming out currently puts all the power in the listeners' hands, and that's not the way it should be.

I take a lot of comfort in knowing that Jesus had to come out, too. Not about his sexuality or gender identity (at least that we know of), but he still needed to reveal something about his identity to the people in his life. Jesus did so as many queer and trans people do: in stages.

I wonder when Jesus first started to realize that he was different than the people around him. That he was called to something greater. That his calling was going to require something of him that he might not have been ready to give. Some people believe that Jesus came out of the womb knowing that he was the Messiah, the Son of

God. I'm not so sure. If Jesus was going to really understand what it means to be human, then he would also need to understand the halting and confusing nature of figuring out who you are and how you want to be in the world.

Jesus started his public ministry and started attracting followers. They started to feel each other out with their own questions. Who is this guy? What kind of movement is this going to be? How fast are we going to move? How much can we change? Even as people left everything to join Jesus's public movement, I'm sure there were questions as they figured out what they were doing and how they were going to be together.

There quickly developed an inner circle and an outer circle. Peter, James, and John stepped into that inner ring. Jesus shared more with them, taught them more directly, gave them more responsibility. And when it came time, they were the first people that Jesus came out to.

One day Jesus goes off to pray alone, as he does often. Some of the disciples join him, and Jesus asks them, "Who do people say that I am?" (Luke 9:18–20) Maybe he's trying to figure out what people are saying about him. What are the rumors? Who is he being compared to? Do people have questions or doubts? Do people believe in him or think he's a fraud? Maybe he needs some confidence to handle what is coming next. To hear what people think so that maybe he won't have to say it out loud. He gets a variety of answers from the trio. "Some say you're a prophet; others think you're John the Baptist come back to life." We can imagine Peter, especially, having a good time with this litany. "Can you believe people? They're so weird!"

I wonder about this conversation. We often read this as a calm, steady, teaching moment. Jesus, the guy in charge, testing his followers. But I read this as a man, alone with his friends, vulnerably asking them who they think he is. "Pete, who am I? James, do you trust me? John, I don't know what's happening, but I think I'm called to something big." The guys quiet down. They realize that something is happening here. It's not time for jokes; it's time to get serious. Peter gathers up his courage. He's been asked a question and this time he wants to get the answer right. He doesn't want to hurt his friend. He wants to acknowledge this moment.

"You are the Messiah. The Son of God."

Does Jesus feel relief? Dread? Fear?

It is out. Out in the open. The words, the seditious words, the words that could get them all killed, have been said out loud. There is silence between them. They're all in it now. This is big. This is the revelation of a new identity. This changes everything. And Jesus immediately shuts it down. He orders all of them not to tell anyone about this conversation.

But then, eight days later, Jesus takes just Peter, James, and John and leads them up a mountain (Luke 9:28–36). It's like he needed those days to gather up his courage. On the walk up the mountain, maybe, like me, he could feel his breathing quicken and his heart start to race. He wants to spend time in prayer, and as he does he starts to transform in front of them. His clothes flash white, he sees Moses and Elijah. His friends are overwhelmed and almost pass out at the sight.

Then the sky splits open, a voice from heaven repeats what was said at Jesus's baptism as if to say, "Duh. You've been this all along! Get with the program!" Jesus's identity is affirmed. It's all rather shocking and overwhelming. The guys fall to their knees, and then when they look up again, it's just them and Jesus. It's just the three of them with this huge shift of reality between them. This moment on the mountain is an invitation to his closest friends to see him even more clearly. It's the step from knowing intellectually that Jesus is the Christ, to knowing experientially what that means.

And what it means is nothing will be the same after this. If Jesus is really the Messiah, that means that everything is about to become real and even more dangerous than it was.

These men who just moments ago heard and held Jesus's identity with such care feel their fear overtaking them. Peter's first thought: "So why don't we just stay here for a while. Hang out. Build some shelters. Camp out." On the surface it seems kind. A marking of space and time. Peter wants to acknowledge the moment, he wants to acknowledge the shift in identity, and he also wants to keep his friend safe. He knows if they move off this mountain they are at risk. Walking off the mountain means walking toward Jerusalem and a confrontation with the powers that be. He wants to slow this train down. Maybe he wants to make sure Jesus really knows what he's doing.

How many transgender people have heard the same? "You've already been living in this body for so long, so why do you need to change it now?" Or "Aren't you too young to be making such life-altering decisions?" Or "Isn't this a little fast? Don't you want some more time to think about it before you do anything drastic?" These questions are asked with concern by the people closest to us. But what those same people don't realize is that even if we're saying these words aloud for the first time, we've almost always been thinking about them for years. By the time we speak our truth aloud we have reached our breaking point, unable to go back or slow down or really do anything but move forward.

Jesus probably felt the same. He'd been walking and working and ministering for a couple of years by the time of the Transfiguration. Continually wrestling with and growing into his calling. He knew the time was coming when his priorities would put him on a collision path with the powers that be. His decision to walk toward Jerusalem wasn't a whim. It wasn't hasty or ill-advised; it was the fruit of his fully leaning into his identity and power. It may have seemed sudden to Peter, but it wasn't to Jesus.

Peter's impulse to build a shelter and keep everyone safe was actually hurtful and harmful to Jesus. It was a spoken doubt at a time when Jesus needed confidence and support. Jesus needed to know that his closest friends were going to back him up and their hesitation to walk with him off the mountain must have been painful. They eventually got on board, but in that moment, every second of delay must have felt like a moment of betrayal.

Coming out is a fragile time. It's a time that invites intimacy but that can lead to wounding. Even the slightest of frowns or hesitations in response can be read as a denial of support. Many people have waited years to reveal this part of themselves and they are rightly sensitive to any kind of rejection. When we invite people into knowing the deepest parts of ourselves, we need to be met with gentleness, love, and an affirmation of unconditional support.

ᘐᘐ

People have a variety of responses when someone comes out. There are those who simply sit in silence and then pretend the words were never spoken. There are those who meet the moment with an affirmation of love and respect but who then struggle to make that love and respect a reality. There are those who meet the moment with anger and rage and others who meet the moment with physical violence. There are parents who throw their children out of the house and others who put their children into conversion therapy. There are parents who insist their children know better and if they just tried harder or prayed more, they could be not queer.

And yes, there are the parents who are kind and loving, who hold space for a coming out moment and assure their children of their love and care, and who back up those words with actions.

Those parents are few and far between, especially in religious homes, and for too long those stories were so rare that even when someone thinks their parent will probably be affirming, there is fear and anxiety leading up to the coming out moment.

It's not just parents or family who bungle responses. There are the moments when we come out to friends and colleagues, church leaders and congregants. At each coming out moment there are different layers of risk, both emotional and practical. If I come out to my family and they kick me out, then I will need to find a new place to live. If I come out to this friend and they reject me, then I will lose my emotional support from them. If I work at a church and come out to leadership there and they fire me, then I will need to find a new job. What if I can't find housing, support, or employment once I've come out? There are so many questions to consider before we even utter the words.

And sometimes the response on the surface seems kind, but there is pain lurking underneath. The parent who accepts their transgender child but insists upon "grieving" the child who was lost (even though their child is still standing in front of them). The spouse who honors their spouse's transition but doesn't want to continue being in a romantic relationship with them. The parents who say they are supportive but struggle to use a new name and pronouns.

When I came out as trans it was such a relief to finally have language for an internal pain that had been dogging me for decades. Now I finally knew what to call it and I knew how to fix it. All of the years of thinking I was broken or that there was something dreadfully wrong with me. All of the years of feeling like I would never be happy in my body, that I would always feel out of place, that no one would ever really see me the way I saw myself. All of the years of agony and isolation—all of it was now given not only language but a way to be relieved. I was ecstatic and ready to change my life.

People were supportive. They affirmed what I was coming to understand about myself. They, too, found the language helpful. They used my pronouns (some faster and more seamlessly than others). They affirmed me. But there was also hesitancy. Questions. Are you moving too fast? Do you need to do this right now? Maybe you should wait. Maybe you should spend some more time in therapy. Maybe you should graduate from seminary first.

I was impatient. After having waited what felt like my whole life to finally come to this realization, I didn't want to wait another second. I felt like I had wasted too much of my life living as someone I wasn't, and I was ready to step into my new understanding and move forward as myself. I was ready to change my pronouns and the way I moved through the world. I was ready to start hormones and access surgery and use the right bathroom. I was ready, and every person who asked a question or raised a concern felt like someone who was rejecting me. It was hard, in those moments, to see that those people, too, were on a journey. And in that particular moment our journeys were both in tandem and on different roads. It was like heading to the same destination on an upper and a lower road. Needing to walk in parallel but not together felt lonely, but I also knew that I couldn't facilitate their process for them. I couldn't answer their questions. I couldn't relieve their fears. All I knew was that I had to make this transition. I had to do it now, and everyone else was going to have to catch up or be left behind.

Some people were left behind. Others did the work to catch up. The process was messy and painful and full of hard conversations. I understood the impulse of my friends to want to build a shelter and keep me safe. I was in seminary and planning to be ordained, but I didn't know how I would make that happen as a transgender person. I didn't know who would want me. I wasn't sure any denomination would. In my friends' minds, encouraging me to slow down, figure out my next steps, and wait a little longer seemed completely reasonable. It might have been, except for someone who had already been waiting for twenty-five years, another second felt like an eternity.

I wonder if Jesus felt the same impatience with his friends after his transfiguration. If their desire to build a shelter and keep him safe might have felt like they were missing the whole point.

Coming out isn't safe. It's inherently risky because of the world we live in. Transgender people face incredible odds when they become themselves. Astronomical rates of violence, poverty, housing discrimination, health care discrimination, educational barriers, and yes, even violence and death might await a transgender person. When someone comes out as transgender, they are taking on incredible risk.[1]

Yet when transgender people don't transition, they face extreme mental health challenges. One of the arguments that trans people shouldn't transition is the concerning rate of suicidality among the community.[2] (Forty percent of transgender people attempt suicide at some point in their lives.) What those statistics miss is that it's not necessarily being transgender that makes someone suicidal. Rather, it's not being accepted or allowed to transition. It's coming out into a world that isn't built for transgender people and a society that wants us, in many corners, not to exist.

And yet, so many transgender people, at younger and younger ages, are facing the risk and coming out. They are declaring the truth about their identity to the world around them. It's beautiful to see. When someone is able to live into their truth, they become a beacon for others to do the same.

One reason people are so strongly drawn to Jesus is his humanity: the depth of it, the way it expanded their own notions of what it means to be human. Jesus was only able to be fully human by also claiming his full divinity. By being all of who he was and declaring that to others. He knew that he was taking a risk and that to claim his identity, walk off that mountain, and set his face toward Jerusalem were risky endeavors. He knew his truth might get him killed, and yet he also knew declaring it was something he had to do.

This knowing—of the truth of ourselves, of the reality of the risk, and of the willingness to live into the truth anyway—is a holy space. When someone invites you into this space, walk as if you are on sacred ground.

Easter Saturday and Easter Sunday: Pain and Power

I thought the worst thing that could happen to me was my marriage ending. And not only to me but to the belief in queer love for my family and friends. When I first came out, I was told over and over again that gay people just cared about sex. They were incapable of forming long-term relationships. They had many partners (sometimes at the same time). Oh, and they were also super depressed, did a lot of drugs, and were all alcoholics.

Even though, as I looked around my new friend group, these stories didn't hold truth, I still had this idea in my head that I had to be the perfect gay Christian in order to convince everyone not only of my goodness but of the goodness of my entire community. I had to prove that I could be just like my evangelical peers: I could wait to have sex until I was married. I could get married. I could go to church and keep my faith and even be a pastor. I would have the "traditional family." It sounds ridiculous to me now, but at the time I was so determined. Even as the marriages of my evangelical friends started to unravel, even as we talked about how so many of us had rushed into lifetime commitments without even knowing ourselves, even as I knew that my marriage didn't carry the same weight as my straight peers' marriages did in the eyes of the church, I still felt all of this pressure to get it right.

This pressure caused me to ignore any relational warning signs I might have been experiencing. From our whirlwind romance to marrying a year later followed almost immediately by me starting seminary, to coming out as transgender a year after that, we had been through a lot together. I told myself that my wife and I were committed to one another, that every relationship had hard times, that we were just stressed out because of money or time or school. But no matter what we did, things didn't seem to get better. Even when we had a bit more money or we could take a weekend off we still struggled to communicate and get along.

I didn't tell anyone about our fights or struggles. I thought I needed to protect our privacy. I thought that to be a good partner meant never, ever complaining, so when I was out with friends I tried to paint a rosy picture of a couple in love. I talked about our future plans. I rushed to get home every night. I missed out on times with my friends, seminary experiences, and experiences in the city in order to take the long train ride home to New Jersey. I didn't talk to others about the fights. I made excuses for my wife's behavior when we were out together. I told myself it would get better; we just needed to weather this patch. There was always another patch, though.

After I came out as trans, we started to see a marriage counselor, a former nun who had come out as a lesbian and was now married to a woman. We thought some outside support would help us navigate my transition, and this therapist's unique identities seemed a good compromise. Here was someone who would understand the religious dynamic and also understand Amy's anxieties as a queer woman. The problem was the therapist didn't entirely understand trans identity. Early in our sessions she had an individual session with each of us. I would learn later that she told Amy in her session that she would eventually leave me. When I found out about this prediction, I felt betrayed by someone we were supposed to trust, someone who was supposed to help us communicate with one another but who instead planted more seeds of doubt.

My seminary graduation was looming and I didn't know what I was going to do next. The therapist couldn't understand my anxieties about finding church work. I had no idea who would hire someone like me. My entire career had been in youth ministry and I felt the demand for queer and trans youth pastors was going to be pretty slim. On the other hand, Amy thought I needed to get a higher paying job than my work as a bartender. I was paying half of all of our expenses, even while in school, but the money never seemed to be enough to get us to a comfortable place. We were always scrambling to pay our rent and have enough left over for food. Amy and the therapist seemed to think my getting a new job as soon as seminary was over was the solution to most of our problems. I wanted to maybe stay at the bar for a little while longer. They thought I was unmotivated, but really, I was afraid. I was still early in my transition. I wasn't always perceived correctly as male. I thought about transitioning and then going "stealth," meaning not talking about my gender identity or transition with people, but I needed time to figure out how I wanted to move through the world. My transition wasn't as simple as everyone else was making it out to be.

I felt alone, but I also felt ashamed, and so I didn't invite anyone to acknowledge my fear or anxiety. When I tried to talk about the conflicted feelings I had about my future job prospects with Amy, I felt unheard and rejected, so I stopped trying. I also didn't feel like I could really talk to my friends because I didn't want to reflect badly on Amy. I had been taught to value privacy, especially around relationship issues. I still carried with me this idea that in order to be acceptable as a queer couple we needed to be perfect. So I hid our relationship's cracks and I spent time with my journal.

I withdrew into myself. I lost my temper at work because I was so stressed. Everything felt like it was pressing in on me and I didn't know what to do.

Looking back on my relationship and marriage, the cracks were there from the beginning; I would have seen them if only I had been taught to trust myself. I thought that intuition was something to be denied because it came from our bodies and our bodies, our flesh, were sinful. My intuition couldn't be trusted because it was telling me the things that the flesh wanted, so I shoved my intuition down and kept pushing forward. I felt I could make the marriage work through sheer force of will. I figured if I just put in the work I could right the ship. I tried to do nice things for Amy, I encouraged therapy for us, I tried to pay for even more things; no matter what I did, it wasn't enough.

As I began my transition, I told myself I needed to do whatever I could to make my wife happy because she was going through something hard. Actually, no—I was putting her through something difficult. This was all my fault. Maybe I was selfish for transitioning. When she would out me as transgender to friends or strangers, I would excuse it because I was trying to be understanding. Intellectually I knew my being seen as male, as who I truly was, felt like it was erasing her lesbian identity. When people saw us together, they made assumptions about both of us that weren't always accurate. I knew it pained her to be seen as something she wasn't. Boy, did I know how that felt. I wanted to spare her from that pain, so over and over I tried to put her needs ahead of my own. That's what I believed a good partner did, after all. That's what I had been taught a good Christian did: we were to put other people's needs first. I remember specifically being taught the acronym JOY: Jesus, Others, You. I was told that's how you found true joy: ignore your needs, put others first, and do whatever it took to be of service to other people. That's what I did. It's what I had been trained to do. It's amazing how often the theology I was taught growing up coalesced with where I was in the present to create an emotionally toxic stew. But no matter how much I put Amy's needs ahead of my own, it didn't seem to work. The distance kept growing between us, the anger kept bubbling up on both sides.

I took that burden on, too. I searched for examples of couples who had made it through a spouse's transition and stayed together. I researched and sent her links. I read books and passed them on to her. I looked for support groups. She would glance at a link and then move on. Go to one support group meeting and leave feeling affirmed in her feelings of betrayal and anger. Scoff at the people who made it. I couldn't see she was already checked out from our marriage. I still believed we could make it. I meant it when I made my marriage vows and I wasn't about to break them.

This refusal to see what was happening cost me. I was so busy trying to hold us together and to meet her needs that I never bothered to ask what my needs were. I never considered the cost of staying. I drifted away from my friends so I could spend more time at home. I was distracted by the weight of the questions, the uncertainty of the future. Every time she criticized me, I thought, "I can do better. I can fix this."

On Easter Sunday morning, just a couple of months before my seminary graduation, Amy told me she was no longer attracted to me and she hadn't been for some time. I was devastated. I didn't know where to turn. I sank even deeper into depression. After that Easter morning revelation we tried one more time to make it work: more therapy, more planning for the future, more covering over the cracks in our relationship. I thought, again, we could turn it around. We made it through my graduation, smiling and seemingly there for each other. We had a nice dinner with friends after the graduation until more stress over money got us fighting again.

In the next couple of weeks things fully unraveled. We were short with one another and money was tight. We were having an argument about bills and rent. Amy was in the kitchen and I was in the bedroom. Amy loudly said, "We need to move into a cheaper apartment when our lease is up."

At that moment, I finally asked the question I should have asked weeks before: "Are we even staying together?"

There was a brief silence, then without coming into the bedroom she simply replied, "No."

That was it. The ending. It was finally decided. She had finally decided. She didn't want this relationship. She didn't want me. I was crushed. I had no idea how to respond.

Neither of us could afford to break our lease or move out, so we decided to live together until August when the lease was up. In hindsight that was a terrible decision, but in the moment, it was all I could think of. I had just graduated from seminary with massive debt. I had only my bartending job and no other prospects. I had zero dollars in savings and no family to fall back on. There was no way that I could move home again; I knew it would kill me.

That summer was awful. My car broke down and I didn't have the money to get it fixed, so I had to count on Amy for rides to and from work. She was often late. One day she decided to go to the beach and stay there past when I needed to be picked up. I got off of work and had no way to get home. I hadn't even made enough money to afford a cab. I sat outside the restaurant and wondered how the hell I had ended up here.

I was afraid to tell my mom about the divorce. I didn't want anyone to know that I had failed. That's what I felt like: a failure. Just another gay person unable to keep a marriage together. Even in the midst of my own deep pain I was thinking about everyone else. What they would think, how they would feel, how would this moment reflect on the entire queer community? This didn't feel like a personal moment between two people; it felt like a very public failure that could set the movement back.

Whether I was a Christian living my witness out in the world, or a queer person reflecting my entire community, my life was never just my own. I couldn't ever simply live without worrying about what everyone else would think. Internalizing those messages—that my life was not my own, that I was a public witness—meant that I prioritized the needs and feelings of other people over myself.

That summer was a moment when I thought surely my story was over. My marriage was done. My savings were gone. I felt like all hope was lost. I had no idea what I'd do next, no idea if I could even continue in ministry. Nothing was working out like I thought it would. I thought once I transitioned, everything would fall into place, and yet there I was, completely broken.

I made some connections with seminary classmates and a friend from a camp I worked at previously and decided to move to Minneapolis. A whole new start in a place where I only knew a few people. I packed what I could fit in a rental car and as I drove away from my home, from my now ex-wife, from any in-person community I had, as I crossed the state line out of New Jersey, I cried. I was terrified. I felt unlovable. I had no idea how I was going to rebuild. Everything seemed fragile and about to shatter.

I drove and cried. I tried to listen to some music, but it felt like every song reminded me of the life I could no longer inhabit. I was driving away, yes, but I was not sure what I was driving toward.

ᴖᴖ

After Jesus's crucifixion, he was taken off of the cross and laid in a tomb. Dead. The men had all scattered (except, maybe, for the Beloved Disciple). Judas was dead.

Chapter 8

The movement was over. The whole thing was done for. Failed.

We often rush to the ending of the story (resurrection). We know what's coming, and so we push past the moments of despair, but we need to sit in them.

Feel the overwhelming despair. Feel the fear. Feel the unknown. Peter and Andrew left their aging father and their entire family business to follow Jesus for three years. Matthew gave up his lucrative job as a tax collector. These men had left families and homes, possibly wives and children. They had given their all for the promise of a revolution and of a new way of being. It wasn't supposed to end like this.

Jesus was dead.

He was not sleeping or passed out or pretending. He was dead. Killed by the empire. Killed by the collusion of religious authorities and government officials who were threatened by the message he brought. Killed like so many other revolutionaries in so many other eras and times. Jesus was dead. The movement was done, and not only was the mission a failure, but the rest of the disciples were probably the next to die. Jesus was the leader, but they were the inner circle. Everyone knew who they were. Peter dodged the guards the night before, but that wouldn't last for very long. They were coming.

The men hid together. Maybe back in the upper room where they had so recently celebrated their last meal together. Where they had been a family. Where the promise had shown so bright. But now they were behind locked doors, lights dim, hiding.

And hurting. Their friend, their leader was dead. He was not coming back. Nothing would be the same again. What were they supposed to do now? Peter thought, "Maybe I could go back to fishing. My father has to take me back into the family business, right? I can do that again, that'll be fine."

Maybe another disciple thought about leaving town, finding another place to settle down. Starting over with a new name. Trying to make some semblance of a life with whatever time he has left.

These were not men who were plotting the movement's next moves, not men who were keen to keep the mission going. These men were afraid and grieving. They were done in. There was no spark left. Jesus had been the glue who held them all together. He was the one with the mission. He had the plans and the vision. They were just the followers. Half of the time they didn't even understand what the hell he was going on about. They didn't have a sense of what this kingdom of God could look like. Maybe they should have never left home. Maybe that whole endeavor had been a waste. Who were they to think they could go up against the Roman Empire and win? Now they would be executed for treason and for what? Nothing had changed. Nothing had changed.

Nothing except them. But had they changed? Not enough. Not enough to keep the message alive, not without Jesus. Jesus was dead.

It can be easy to rush to the resurrection, to tell these men to just hold on for a couple of days, but as day turns into night, into day, into night again, there was nothing but despair. They didn't know anything else was coming. They simply hid.

In some Christian traditions, there is a belief that Jesus spends this in-between time "harrowing hell": rescuing prisoners and setting the captives free. He is a warrior defeating Satan in the place where he lives and leading everyone out with him. It's a nice image. Comforting in that even in the moments where we think all is lost, Jesus is actually still getting shit done. It's a picture that fits our active American psyches. Kick ass; take names. Jesus as triumphant warrior. American Christianity is much more comfortable with this image of Jesus than a Jesus who was simply dead. The triumphant Jesus is too easy to promote; this picture pushes us past our uncomfortable feelings into ones of triumph and winning. What if, though, Jesus was just dead? What if everything was, indeed, lost? What would that do to our faith? How do we handle the moments when God is absent and there's no plan and we can't even remember what it is that we're supposed to be working toward? Those days when we can't see the larger vision and it feels like even the idea of the kingdom of God is just a dream that will never survive in the harsh light of day.

What of those Easter Saturdays in our lives? The day when we realize our marriage is over. The moment when the doctor delivers the terminal diagnosis. The funeral of our child, or worse, the day after the funeral of our child, when the silence that settles into the house is a silence deeper than we have ever experienced before. The moment when we realize the faith we once had is gone and it's not coming back. The moment we realize institutions where we've placed our hope weren't to be trusted.

We sit in the silence of the despair. The bleak place where we struggle to find the way forward. Some would call this a liminal space, in between what was and what is to come. To even get to the liminal, we need to believe there is hope on the other side, a way through the desolation, and as we sit in Easter Saturday hope is nowhere to be found.

In many of our churches we skip Easter Saturday. The church that I grew up in skipped Good Friday, too. We observed Palm Sunday and then skated right on over to Easter. (We also rushed from the birth of Jesus to his death on the cross without ever talking about the message he brought during his life on Earth.) Some churches observe the Easter vigil (the Saturday night leading into Easter Sunday), but many churches strip the altar on Good Friday and then walk in to flowers and horns and shouts of "Alleluia!" on Easter morning. We rush over the unknown. We skim over the grief. We live with the security of the spoiler of knowing how it's all going to turn out.

Life doesn't come with the same guarantee. We don't always know there is something better on the other side of the hell we are currently living in. I certainly didn't. My Easter Saturday wasn't just my marriage ending; it was my physical transitioning beginning as well. Those two major life moments wrapped around each other, complicating each other.

For the first year of my medical transition, I take photos every month. Photos of my face staring at the camera, of my face from the side, of my torso and back. I'm tracking the most minuscule changes. Does my jaw line look just a bit more chiseled? Do my hips look less wide? Is my hairline shifting at all? Is that smudge on my lip, the one that only shows up in the flash, the beginnings of a mustache? I record my voice to hear how it's changing. I need to know my patience is going to pay off, that even though my changes are slow changes are still occurring. I am paying attention to my body with a level of detail I haven't bothered with since my first puberty. This time around I am approaching these changes with joy instead of praying they would stop.

I scour the internet for photos from guys who are farther along in their transitions. I want to see what I have to look forward to. I want reassurance this is going to work for me, that I can live the life I've been longing for. What did other people experience one month in? Two months? Seven? When did they stop getting misgendered when they went to the store? On the phone? How did their families and partners react? Was I going to be okay?

Am I going to be okay? That is the question that keeps me up at night. As I have hard conversation after hard conversation with my wife. As I wait for the next harsh email or letter from my mother. As I consider the future of where I might find a job, where I might get ordained, if anyone will ordain me.

I worry that no one will want me. It's a visceral fear. It goes beyond just worrying about employment to fearing I will lose everyone and everything. Will my wife still want me? Will my family still want me? Will my friends still want me? Will there be any place at all for me in this world?

I learned from my childhood and teenage years in the evangelical church these were valid questions. If you stepped out of line, if you asked the wrong questions (or sometimes any questions at all) and if you didn't conform, there was a very good chance there wouldn't be space for you. Not in the leadership team, not in the small group, not in your own family. While I had freed myself from those constricting theological tenets, the fear they had ingrained in me was still strong.

The problem is, these fears weren't all in my head. A quick Google search for "my partner is transgender" will give you page after page after page of internet sites where cisgender partners talk about how hard it is to love someone trans. Page after page of comments saying, "Your marriage will never survive this," and "You'll have to leave them." Page after page of people calling transgender people selfish for being ourselves. I know, because I read them. I went looking for hope my marriage could survive, that there were examples out there I could emulate. I went looking for reassurance and found despair. Those messages—that I was selfish, that it was so hard to love me—wormed themselves into my heart right next to all of the messages from my childhood that said it was so hard for God to love a terrible sinner like me.

Most branches of evangelicalism prime you to accept abusive language and behavior because it's baked into the theology: God needed to kill God's son in order to even look at you. God wants to throw you in hell if you don't repent. You are to suffer with joy because it's what God wants. No wonder I read those online messages of guaranteed rejection and thought, "Yeah, I really am hard to love." I read those messages and when my wife did hurtful things I thought, "I deserve this because I am ruining her life." When she outed me without my permission, or made jokes about my body, or blamed me for every fight I just took it because, after all, I had chosen to transition. I was the one betraying her with my decision to pursue my own truth.

Even as I knew, in my deepest being, that my transition wasn't a mistake—it was necessary and lifesaving—it was hard to disentangle doubts as my marriage crashed around me, as I walked into work and still wasn't allowed to use the men's restroom, as customers and other staff used a jumble of pronouns for me. Was this how my life was turning out? And as my transition progressed, I wondered if this was all there is. I was divorced, working crappy jobs, misgendered repeatedly, mostly ignored by my family, and I had no money and no safe place to live. Was this it? Was this all that was left for me?

And if so, would it be worth it?

ᗡᗞ

Before Jesus's crucifixion, the disciples had had a vision in their heads of what the future looked like: triumphant, powerful. They had dreams of who they would be in this new movement: the ones with power, the people in charge. No more oppression. No more subjugation. No more. Then Jesus died, and everything the disciples had envisioned went away. There was no backup plan. No alternative vision.

With the hindsight of knowing the whole story we can call the disciples weak or say they lacked faith. We can chide them for missing the point of what Jesus taught as soon as he was dead. We can decide they didn't listen well enough and therefore were caught unawares. But perhaps they were simply being human. The disciples were people whose lives had just been upended. People whose hope had been shattered. Had we been the disciples, would we have acted any differently?

How often have we lost the plot because we thought we knew how the story ended? How often have we gotten off track because we were so determined to make things happen the way we wanted them to (even if it killed us!)?

On Easter Saturday, we are stuck in the waiting. There is a required passivity. But I think there is another way to understand what is happening on this day.

We struggle with believing in a powerless Jesus. A vulnerable Jesus. We struggle with the terror of the unknown because many of us prefer to be in control and live our lives accordingly. Western Christians don't live in an occupied country. We are relatively free. We can vote and travel and move about. For a lot of American Christians especially, the Covid-19 pandemic beginning in 2020 was the first time they felt a sense of vulnerability, a sense when everything was very much not in control. We saw how different groups of Americans reacted, screaming about hoaxes and the curtailing of citizens' rights when masks were mandated. We saw how unwilling people were to think about their neighbors' needs or safety. We saw how scarcity mindsets kicked in and toilet paper was hoarded.

Yet for people who have often lived on the margins—trans people, Black people, Indigenous people, People of Color, queer people, people with disabilities—we know what it's like to be vulnerable. We know what it's like to be at risk. We know what it's like to feel that impactful decisions are made without us or our representatives in the room. We struggle against systems that seek to actively oppress us.

We live in the same America and yet we don't have the same freedom of movement. We struggle to gain access to the things other people take for granted.

We resonate strongly with a God who knows what it's like to be powerless and vulnerable. A God who knows what it's like to wait. A God who needs to be resurrected. I resonate with a God who understands what it's like to have the people who are closest to you run away in your time of need. I want a God who knows what it's like to have to face your hardest moments alone and without access to resources. A God who knows what it's like to be in a tomb for a while.

Easter Saturday serves as a powerful and provocative message of prolonged waiting, even today. It is our reminder to sit with our pain and despair, to face it head on and not run from it. It is a reminder that even in the midst of the despair, God—Jesus—knows how it feels.

The Kingdom of God: Courage to Be

One of the patterns in my life has been staying too long. I used to call it tenacity or following through, but now I understand it to be rooted in something else: people pleasing and an inability to listen to my own gut. There have been times when I tried to make relationships work way longer than I should have. Jobs, churches, even a marriage where I was so determined to stay that I ignored the damage it was doing to my body and soul. I wanted to do the right thing. I wanted to be faithful and I wanted to fulfill my promises. I ignored the warning messages that contradicted the life I felt I was supposed to be living.

Growing up in the evangelical church I was taught to distrust myself. Not just my physicality, but also my mind. We were taught we were fragile people, riddled through with a sin nature. Everything we wanted to do was evil and wrong. If we desired something, those desires weren't to be trusted. When you couple those teachings with the culture of dismissiveness toward anyone who grew up in a female body, you have a recipe for disaster. Intuition, our God-given gift to help us protect ourselves in dangerous situations, is seen as something to be ignored instead of as the gift it is. Pushed aside. Dismissed.

Many people are still taught that our intuition will lead us astray. That still small voice that warns you this adult volunteer isn't safe? Ignore it. Chalk it up to Satan trying to keep you from respecting your leaders. The voice that screams to you that this situation is dangerous? Ignore it, and know that fear must be distracting you from following God. This sense of deep truth that tells you who you are and who you love? It's not from God, so you need to fight against it. These messages I was taught in my youth continued into adulthood.

I stayed in relationships because I was trying to "obey God." I stayed in jobs because I kept ignoring the voice telling me to get out. If there was something, anything I wanted, I told myself I wasn't allowed to have it. I didn't use certain personal talents because they came too easily. I made things harder and harder on myself because I thought that suffering was how you developed holiness.

Everything good was supposed to come from outside of us, which makes us ripe for being controlled by others. If you're taught you can't trust yourself and that God speaks through leaders, then you ignore the twinges of doubt when the preacher says something that doesn't make sense. If you're taught that your own desires mean nothing, you choose to enter into a relationship with the "right" person you may feel nothing for, and you call that holiness. If you desire someone or something beyond the acceptable norms, you run the other way, because surely that must be Satan tempting you.

I waited to come out initially because I was afraid of what my mother would think and worried about how it would impact my ministry. I waited to come out again and transition because I feared what it would cost me personally and professionally. I ignored the warning signs in my marriage because I felt like I was already too far in to leave. Over and over again, I pushed my own needs to the side in order to live up to other people's expectations and standards.

I couldn't wrap my head around the fact that I mattered, too. I ignored my own needs and desires until I couldn't even name what I needed anymore.

I didn't know how to set boundaries. I didn't know how to ask for what I needed. I didn't feel like I had any agency in my own life. Things happened to me and I let them happen. I was unhappy, but I did nothing to change my situation because I didn't feel like I could. I waited to be outed. I waited for jobs to cut me loose. I was passive, and my passivity was killing me. But it was more than just a bent toward being passive—it was an internalizing of my powerlessness.

I had been taught over and over again that God was in control, that what I wanted didn't matter, that God was going to do with me what God wanted whether I liked it or not. God would make things happen to me so I would be and do better. If I didn't obey, then God would punish me to bring me back into line; so, in a lot of respects, it didn't matter what I did because God was in control.

Then as a trans person, I internalized all sorts of messages about what kind of life was available to me. I read the stories about trans people being more likely to live in poverty, to be victims of violence, to face job and housing insecurity. I saw the news reports of the continual assaults on trans people's right to exist in public, from bathroom laws, to laws about changing documents, to laws about discrimination in public accommodations.[1] At every turn I heard the loud and vociferous voices calling for my expulsion from the public sphere. I saw how even members of the LGB community would toss aside transgender people if it meant that they could be protected.

Closer to my home life, I internalized the messages about how hard it was to love transgender people. I read articles, looking for some kind of hope that I could transition and keep my marriage intact, but hope was hard to find. Instead of standing up for myself, I took online messages about relationship struggles for trans people as a sign that there was something wrong with me, that I was the problem in our relationship.

When I realized I was transgender, when I finally said the words to myself, it was like my entire life finally made sense. All of those experiences I'd had—the euphoria from playing King David as a boy, my love of baseball caps, the desire for short hair—it all made sense. Even more deeply felt was my sense that, since puberty, something had been wrong. Off kilter. Not right. Something that I could never quite put my finger on but that pervaded my every day. Something that wasn't fixed when I came out as gay (even though I had hoped it would be). When I said, "I think I might be transgender," then everything clicked into place. Oh, THIS is the reason I've felt like this. THIS is the reason I struggle with gendered spaces. This is the reason something feels off about my body. This, this, this.

When I finally allowed my intuition to resurface it was like breathing again after being underwater for just a little too long. It was a wave of relief. It was a deep knowing. It was my body telling my mind, "You finally got it." Acknowledging this reality was just that: an acknowledgment of what I had known for years but hadn't had language for.

For people who didn't know me well, my transition might have looked fast. The amount of time from coming out as transgender to starting hormones was about nine months, but to me, all of it simply felt like catching up. My brain was catching up to what my body had always known.

Even in that deep knowing I still had to convince others. I signed up for therapy in order to get a letter saying I was ready to transition medically. In New York, where I was attending seminary at the time, you could start taking hormones without a letter. Medical transition is available simply by informed consent, which means after meeting with a social worker and being told the effects of hormone therapy, you can sign off on your own treatment. I thought about doing that, but my then-wife wanted me to go to therapy first. I'm a big proponent of therapy generally, so I figured it couldn't hurt.

In order to begin hormone therapy, I started seeing a therapist at the LGBT Center in New York. We spent most of our three months together talking about my family, my faith, and my future. It was clear to her I was transgender. She understood that my hang-ups weren't about the rightness of transition but were about what everyone else around me would think and how they would react. I was worried I was making the wrong decision not because I had doubts about my identity, but because I was worried about everyone else. It was already difficult to consider working for a church as an out gay person; what congregation would ever hire someone who was transgender? My wife and I were already struggling to get along; would our relationship survive my transition? Things were already rocky relationally with my mother; would this be the thing to cause her to finally cut off contact and not allow me to see my siblings anymore? I fretted. I panicked. I thought about everyone's needs and desires but my own.

I thought about what my queer friends would think. Would they believe I was selling out the lesbian community? Choosing to transition just to get male privilege? Choosing to transition because it was "easier" for me (in their minds) than staying as I was?

I wondered if I could just stay as I was. I was already moving through the world as a gender nonconforming person. Maybe I didn't really need to medically transition. I'd already survived twenty-six years as someone who lived outside of "traditional" femininity; I could surely survive more. Maybe I should just stay as I was. Make everyone else happy. Not trouble the water.

I went back and forth, turning it over and over in my mind. As I neared the end of the three months of therapy and even as I made appointments for my pre-transition lab work, I still wondered. One day I became still and quiet and checked in with myself and I felt—deeply—that even if the worst happened—even if my wife left me, even if I had to leave the ministry, even if my family disowned me—I had to do this. There was no real choice. It was either do this or never be fully myself. I had to move forward. Now that I knew the truth I couldn't un-know it. Now that I felt this truth in my body, I had to do what was right for me even if no one else understood. Even if it cost me everything.

The day I was scheduled to get my very first shot of testosterone and begin my medical transition, I was nervous and on edge. I was terrified something would go wrong; maybe the doctor wouldn't write the prescription, or maybe the pharmacy would be out of stock. My then-wife and I took the train into the city and I was edgy. I was moody and silent. In the back of my mind was also the worry, "What if this is the wrong decision?"

We got to my appointment early at Callen-Lorde, the LGBTQ+ health center in New York City. Then we waited. I always had to wait, it seemed. The clock seemed to move in slow motion as I waited for my appointment time. It came. And went. Still nothing. I was getting more and more nervous as I knew the clinic would be closing at 8 p.m. and we still had to fill the prescription at the pharmacy. I worried that after all this worrying, I wouldn't even be able to get the shot. Finally, I was called back. My paperwork was in order. My labs showed I needed to cut down on cholesterol and sugar, but other than those things everything was good to go. The doctor wrote me a prescription, but now we were in a race with the clock. My then-wife ran to CVS to get it filled, while I stayed put. They held the door open for her so she could get back in. A nurse kept me laughing and at ease as he prepared me for my first shot. Just like that, it was done.

As we stepped back out into the New York night all of my anxiety was gone. A relief flooded my body. I knew, just knew this was the right decision. I never had a second thought again.

We traveled to a restaurant where a group of my friends had gathered. We handed out blue bubblegum cigars that said, "It's a boy!" Someone asked if we were celebrating a birthday. We all laughed, and I said, "I guess we kinda are."

ᴏᴏ

What were you taught about your body growing up? What messages did you internalize? Messages about being pure and modest? About being too much or not enough? About how you should be weak so men could protect you? About how you should be strong and protect others and never show weakness? Were you taught to keep your skin covered, that a bare shoulder or a glimpse of stomach skin could lead people astray? Or were you told it didn't matter what you wore, and that all you had to do was show up and people would let you lead?

Were you taught to trust your body or to fear it?

I was taught to fear mine. I was taught that my body was something I needed to tame, to bring under the control of the people in charge of me. I was to tame my body through modesty. Through purity. I was taught not to let anything in my mind that could pollute me: no bad language or sex scenes in movies, no hints of queerness or gender diversity in books or other media. I was taught that I couldn't trust my desires or dreams. I believed that if I really wanted something it was probably just a temptation from Satan and that I should push it away. I should only do the things I didn't want to do because those were the things from God. My relationship with desire, with intuition, and with trusting myself was all out of balance. I pushed aside the internal voices I should have been listening to and followed external validation, something I should have been ignoring. I didn't know who I was or even how to find out. For so long I'd been told that everything I wanted was wrong. I shouldn't want to be with women. I shouldn't want to be a man. I shouldn't want to be a leader or a pastor. I shouldn't want recognition for my work. I shouldn't expect to have a comfortable life or even to have enough resources. I couldn't trust my body to tell me what I wanted.

I had to relearn to trust myself. To trust my instincts and intuition. To learn to trust that my body would tell me what was good and right. That I would know, in my body, when I was doing the right thing and that my body would warn me when something was off.

I wasn't separate from my body. My brain wasn't at war with my body. They were designed to work together, to be in harmony. These ideas of flesh and spirit being at war with one another weren't the truth; the truth instead was, "The kingdom of God is within you." (Those words from the Gospel of Thomas helped me unlock this truth, as I will discuss below.) Within each one of us is what we need to know to find our purpose, but even more importantly, to find our healing. The work of spirituality became, for me, a journey back to myself. A journey back to trusting my body. It was a journey of unlearning all of the ideas that pushed me off the track. To unlearn modesty and purity as they were presented to me, because those ideas weren't about anything more than other people having control over my body. I had to unlearn the beliefs that told me that sex was sinful and wrong, and that queer sexuality, especially, was the worst kind of sexuality. I had to unlearn ideas about pleasure and understand that it was okay to feel good in my body, not just during sex but in the day-to-day; it was okay to eat good food and enjoy it, it was okay to feel pleasure in putting on my favorite shirt and jeans that fit just right, it was okay to luxuriate in a bath or under blankets just out of the dryer. My body wasn't my enemy—it was good. We were partners. We were one.

Do you remember the first time you were taught to distrust yourself? Maybe you got a weird vibe from a new coworker but everyone else loved him. Maybe you were forced to kiss or hug a relative you didn't want to hug. Was there a moment when someone told you what you were experiencing wasn't real or didn't matter? What did that experience do to your sense of self? How did it impact how you move through the world?

For many of us who were raised evangelical, who grew up queer and/or trans, or who were assigned female at birth, these experiences came early and often. A sense of unease, a sense where what we knew to be true about ourselves and the world was unacceptable to the people around us. We learned how to keep things hidden: certain gestures or turns of phrase, certain articles of clothing, certain desires. We learned to listen to others and ignore ourselves when we had decisions to make. We learned to follow the rules and do the "right" things.

Some of us married early because we were told we were supposed to. Some of us denied our calls to ministry because we were taught that we were unworthy to minister. Some of us ignored the truth about our bodies because we didn't see a future for ourselves. We did all of this ignoring in the name of truth and righteousness. We did it because we thought it was what God wanted. We did it because we were trying to put God and the church first.

Some of us managed to live those lies for years, maybe even decades, but something persisted. The voice inside of us could still be heard even if it was just a whisper instead of the shout it had once been. We tried to avoid hearing the whisper. We prayed harder, we served in more ministries, we had more kids and busied ourselves with raising them right. We read our Bibles and listened to praise music. But the whisper inside persisted.

At some point a breakdown occurred. Maybe you went on a retreat and finally heard the truth you'd been avoiding for so long, maybe you met someone and fell heartrendingly in love for the first time, maybe you made yourself sick with secrets or alcohol, maybe the things you kept hidden away were uncovered in a closet or a trunk or in your internet search history. Suddenly you were thrust into the light and forced to face the pain of all of the hiding.

What if you knew, deep down, that the hiding was never what God wanted for you? What if you could believe there was another way to live, one that would bring freedom and abundance instead of shame and captivity?

ᴖᴗ

There are a series of gospels and other writings that were left out of our traditional biblical canon. They are collections written by early Jesus followers that didn't make the cut determined by the councils of the early church. Some noncanonical gospels have been found in fragments with large portions missing, others are clearly fantastical and not rooted in reality, but some of them are collections of sayings that are provocative and powerful and echo, in slightly different form, things recorded in the gospels considered canonical.

Some people find reading these gospels dangerous; after all, they were left out of the canon for a reason, right? When you read some of the questionable reasons for texts being left out of the canon (there should only be four gospels because there are four pillars holding up the earth, for instance), you wonder what other texts were discarded without good reason. These texts were developed in community, some of the earliest communities of believers who were trying to make sense of what the Jesus story meant to them. They were grappling with how to live out their faith, how to understand the stories about Jesus passed down to them, and how to live in the world. They were trying to understand how to be humans in communion with the Divine. Their recorded struggles are worth paying attention to. The way they articulated their understandings can shed new light on the gospels we are more familiar with.

One of the noncanonical gospels, attributed to Thomas, is a collection of sayings. Two of these sayings, sayings 3 and 70, brought a lot of comfort to me in my early transition and continue to impact me today. These sayings don't contradict the recorded stories and words of Jesus found in the canonical gospels; they simply present truths in a different way. The earliest Christian community was grappling with what the kingdom of God meant. What did it look like? How were they to live it out? What would it feel like when it arrived?

Saying 3 of the Gospel of Thomas reads:[2]

> Jesus said, "If those who lead you say to you, 'See, the kingdom is in the sky,' then the birds of the sky will precede you. If they say to you, 'It is in the sea,' then the fish will precede you. Rather, the kingdom is inside of you, and it is outside of you. When you come to know yourselves, then you will become known, and you will realize that it is you who are the sons of the living father. But if you will not know yourselves, you dwell in poverty and it is you who are that poverty."

One can understand how such a saying might be considered threatening to the councils who were trying to codify and organize the early Christian moment. The writer of this saying is encouraging people to listen to the Spirit inside of them. They were encouraging people to listen to the still small voice, the intuition, the knowing we all carry deep in our bodies about what is true.

Saying 70 reads:

"If you bring forth what is within you, what you bring forth will save you. If you do not bring forth what is within you, what you do not bring forth will destroy you."

When I read this saying, I felt it on a deep level. I understood it in my body because I had experienced it. I know what my life was like before my transition, when I was trying so hard to fit in, to be "normal," to abide by the things expected of me. I know the quality of my relationships before my transition, the way I was never fully present, the ways I held back my affection, the distance I put between myself and others. I truly believe had I not transitioned, at some point my life would have become unbearable and there's a good chance I would have died. That's not hyperbole; it's a deep knowing. Continuing to resist what I knew to be true would have destroyed me. When I had the clarity and the courage to bring forth my truth, only then was I able to become fully myself and be fully in community.

These two sayings, put together, send a message to us to trust what we know to be true. When you know yourselves, when you bring forth what is within you, then you will be known. The flip side, though, if you don't bring forth what is within you it will destroy you. If you hide from the truth, if you keep it pushed down, if you don't reveal yourself to other people—it will eventually destroy you.

This isn't just about gender or sexuality, it could be family secrets or patterns, shifting beliefs in a place where a shift in belief isn't accepted, the realization that you are no longer a good match for your partner. It could be the mental health issue you don't want to face, or any number of other things you know to be true but struggle to find the courage to talk about. These things will make you sick.

This isn't some kind of self-help substitute for the gospel. It's not self-actualization at the expense of holiness. It's instead a recognition that without fullness of being we aren't able to work for justice. Without an understanding of our wholeness, of our belovedness, of God's desire for our abundance, we are unable to see the same in and for others. This is what Jesus is talking about when he says in John 10:10, "The thief enters only to steal, kill, and destroy. I came so that they could have life—indeed, so that they could live life to the fullest." An abundant life, life to the fullest, isn't merely some promise of heaven when we die; rather, it's an assurance that us living into the fullness of our humanity is a good thing. We were given gifts and talents, identities and ways of seeing, particularities that are a dimension and a window onto the face of God. Hiding those particularities harms us and our neighbors. When people are able to be wholly and fully alive, such beauty pours out. When whole communities are able to be wholly and fully alive? Then we start to experience the kingdom of God here and now, among us.

What are the things within you begging to be brought forth? What of your fullness have you been hiding? What are the things you long to say?

What if, when people looked at Christians and churches, instead of seeing folks who were fearful of change, threatened by new identities, and barricaded in their buildings, they saw communities full of people who were fully alive? Communities encouraging the flourishing of all people. Communities making space for diversity. Communities with individuals so healthy they aren't threatened by change or difference, but instead embrace it because they know it will lead to further growth. How different would people's perceptions of Christianity and Christians be? How different would our cities and towns and communities be?

Communities are made up of individuals, so if the individuals are unhealthy, then so is the community. If individuals have a scarcity mindset, a fear of any differences inside themselves, a fear of change, then the community will have those as well. If an individual feels stifled, then a community will feel it as well. If we want our communities to be healthy, then we have to encourage the flourishing of individuals. This isn't to say we focus on people instead of systems, but it is acknowledging that our systems are made of people.

I wasn't able to really be present with other people until I was able to be present with myself. I wasn't able to show up for other people well until I felt secure enough to show up for myself. When I brought forth the knowledge I had been hiding—about my sexuality, about my gender identity—only then was I able to be present and work for justice for other people. It seems counterintuitive, but only once I was able to focus on bringing forth my own truth was I then able to make space in my life to be wholly present for others. I had to get out of my own head, stop worrying about what everyone else thought, but I could only do that once I was present in my body.

How many of the challenges we're facing today are a result of people who aren't fully alive? Who are so concerned with hiding their own faults they cannot be present for others? Our systems are unjust, yes, but so are individuals who cannot make space for others. Individuals who lash out and try to kill those whom they don't understand. Individuals who feel threatened by the people around them simply for existing. Individuals who cannot stand to see joy and brilliance come from marginalized communities because they somehow haven't allowed themselves to unlock what they carry inside.

The idea of the kingdom of God isn't just in the Gospel of Thomas. It's all through the canonical gospels, but many of us miss it because of how we've been taught to understand the Jesus story. We were taught that the overarching message of Jesus was always, always that Jesus came to get people to believe in him so that when he died, we would trust in him for our salvation. But Jesus tells us over and over that his ministry isn't about a change in belief system alone; it's about a change in how we live. It's about a change in priorities and values. It's about a drastically different world order.

It's a threatening message to those in power. It's a whole lot easier to preach about getting saved and going to heaven when you die than it is to consider that the kingdom of God could be here, now, if we would all work for it. The kingdom of God is scary for people who are comfortable, who have privilege and power. It's no wonder Jesus attracted fishermen and women, people who were oppressed and under occupation. Those people had nothing to lose. A new world order might give them a chance, a hope. And if they died? Well, they weren't really living, so what would dying matter?

Jesus's message appeals to those with nothing to lose because people with something to lose are terrified at the thought of what they might have to give up. Even if they'd be better off when all is said and done, the transition period feels overwhelming and terrifying. So people turn Jesus's political message into a spiritual one. They focus on saying the right words and believing the right things because that's less threatening than changing the entire social order. It's easier to say "I prayed this prayer and so I will get to go to heaven when I die" than to understand that my salvation is bound up with the salvation of others and that it depends on being lived out in the here and now. Transgender and queer people, especially those who are further marginalized by their race or socioeconomic status, better understand this communal salvation because it's the way we have survived.

Queer and transgender people are continually sharing what little they have, passing the same $25 around their social circle so that no one goes hungry until payday. We throw parties for one another to raise funds for lifesaving surgery that insurance companies refuse to cover. We take turns giving and receiving because we know that we need each other to get by. Jesus's message comes through loud and clear for us, and when we see the early church described in Acts 2:44–45, it looks familiar: "All the believers were united and shared everything. They would sell pieces of property and possessions and distribute the proceeds to everyone who needed them."

We see that they shared all things in common; we read those verses and say, "Yup, that sounds about right." We recognize ourselves in this story.

Which is why so many of us feel more connection to the spiritual in our queer and trans communities than we feel in the church. We enter into churches where everyone sits in "their" pew and greets one another politely. We see people return to their houses in the suburbs with lots of room, where they don't have to be too close to the muck and grime of the city. They want their churches to be diverse and grow, but only if it means they don't have to give up any of the material things or traditions they love.

We can see that our disconnection from Jesus's message is not just about our churches; it's about our entire society, of which many of the churches are a symptom. The white mainline congregation that still meets in a building in the inner city but whose members all live in the suburbs echoes the police department whose officers patrol those same city streets and then go home to houses outside of the city. Both the church and the police see themselves as separate from their neighbors because, in reality, they are not neighbors. They don't live in the same area, and therefore they don't live in the same reality.

So when I think about the kingdom of God, I see it as both an internal and an external shift. It's people fully alive who build communities of justice. I see room for all sorts of identities. It has room for all people to live an abundant life. The kingdom of God can hold the complexity of all people. Not everyone needs to look the same in the kingdom of God. Not everyone needs to behave in the same way. We can encourage diversity not simply with lip service, but in actuality. We can make space for each of our particularities to be in community with each other.

There is no scarcity in the kingdom of God. There is no uniform in the kingdom. There is no "right way" to believe or behave. There is space for all sorts of traditions and attire. We can bring all of ourselves to the table and know we will be met with welcome and love and the table will be overflowing with food enough for all.

The kingdom of God is within us and among us, if only we have the courage to bring forth what will save us.

CHAPTER 10

Resurrection: New Beginnings

n the summer after my marriage ended, but before I had moved out of our shared home, I was trying to pack my life into boxes. I was working to unmerge all of the things we had merged. Our CDs and DVDs, our bookshelf and kitchen supplies. Moving from an "us" to a "me" again was painful. I had been doing most of the sorting and packing, but as my move-out day approached, I asked Amy to sort the silverware. I had a work shift and the truck was coming in just a couple of days. She kept putting it off and I kept asking. One night while I was out, she finally went through the silverware. I came home to discover what she had set aside for me and there in the bin were all of the mismatched pieces: the slightly bent knives, the spoons neither of us really liked, and the worst part? Four forks. Four. I broke down in tears. She couldn't understand why I was so upset.

It wasn't about the forks, not really. It was the feeling behind it. I was trying to leave the relationship well. I had spent the entire summer making sure she left our relationship with a better house set up than when she entered our home together, and she wasn't doing the same for me. Four forks weren't enough to start over with. In the moment I saw those forks, I realized she didn't care what happened to me next. She was not setting me up for success; she was taking what she could and exiting. My well-being was no longer her concern. Seeing the forks was the final straw. They represented the moment when I realized it was really, truly over.

After I moved to Minneapolis, I spent my first few months wallowing. I managed to get a part-time job doing youth work at a church and I got a job at a bookstore, but money was tight and I was always worried about making it to my next paycheck. I slept on an air mattress with a hole in it, so every night, in the middle of the night, I had to get up and fill it up again. When I scrounged some money to buy a new air mattress it, too, deflated. In the midst of all of the pain, I couldn't see a way out. I didn't know how to take ownership of my life as a newly single adult. Everything was simply happening to me. Every time I would run out of clean forks, I would remember that moment in the kitchen in New Jersey. I would feel the despair all over again and know that I was unloved.

This wasn't what I expected my life to be like. This wasn't how I envisioned my world post transition. Sure, people were using the right pronouns for me now, but everything else still hurt.

It took me several months, but finally I went to the store and bought a couple of packs of forks. They were only a couple of dollars, but the emotional benefit was huge. I decided I was never again going to run out of forks. This was the moment when I decided I was going to take care of myself and make sure I had what I needed. It was time to start over.

In hindsight, our divorce was the best decision for both of us. My transition was an easy scapegoat; we could blame the divorce on shifting identities. I could take on the blame, as had often been the case in our marriage, and she could walk away feeling justified. In hindsight I should have left earlier. There had been red flags well before my transition. So many things are clearer now, but as we walked through the mess together, we were doing the best we could with the information and resources we had at the time. Sometimes they just weren't enough.

Resurrection must start with a death. Sometimes the time spent in the tomb is a lot longer than three days. My Easter Saturday included my transition, but it also encompassed the death of my marriage. It took several years of waiting for things to feel settled, for my body to feel right. It was burying all of my hopes and dreams and starting over again in Minnesota. It was the reconfiguring of the future I had hoped for.

A year or so after I moved to Minnesota, I tried dating. That didn't go so well. The process made me anxious and frantic. I worried about how to come out as trans to potential dates, I worried about my religious background, I worried that I would find another woman who couldn't see me as a man. I messaged some people on dating apps and went on one date before deciding this whole thing felt entirely too stressful.

Instead, I thought I would give celibacy a try, not because I was ashamed of my gender or sexuality or believed that being sexual was wrong, but because I wanted my limited energy to go somewhere else. My energy was limited because the stress of three years of seminary, a marriage filled with strife and fighting, coming out (again), transitioning, and moving my entire life to a new state had taken a significant toll. I hadn't realized how exhausted I was. How stressed out. How pushed to all of my limits. There were weeks when I only went to work, came home, and read books. I watched TV by myself. I slowly, slowly stitched my heart back together.

Celibacy was a temporary solution (for me it lasted six years). It gave me the space to focus on healing. I took the pressure off of myself to meet other people. My experiment with celibacy actually taught me a lot about hospitality. I was able to show up for people in a different way without romance clouding things. When there were clear boundaries, when we were all sure dating wasn't a part of the equation, we could be intimate in different ways. I could hold platonic space for people's hopes and dreams, for their needs, for their hearts. I was able to set aside any crushes or romantic feelings I had because I knew I wanted to show up differently for that person. This freedom created deep and lasting friendships. Some people I tried to get to know didn't understand. They thought I was being silly or living in shame; they believed I was acting out of my hurt and that one day I would be in another relationship. I wasn't so sure. I wasn't eliminating the idea. I said if the right person showed up that I'd be willing to date, but at that point, I didn't want to spend my time and energy going after such a person. My response was, "If God puts someone in my life, then great; otherwise, I am happy to be celibate." I really, truly meant it, and it allowed me to heal and grow. I am so grateful for that time.

Resurrection isn't a moment; it's a process.

In the transition phase of my extended Easter Saturday, I kept thinking that I knew what resurrection looked like. In my mind, resurrection in my personal life looked like a restored marriage. A renewed love and trust between my wife and me. It looked like laughter and joy. It looked like both of us claiming our identities and supporting each other. Since that was my goal, I didn't consider any other options. I just kept fighting and pushing and struggling to make the dying marriage work.

When I pictured resurrection with my family specifically, it looked like them accepting my identity, using the right pronouns for me, and honoring my relationships.

Sometimes resurrection looks different than you anticipated. Sometimes what you had hoped for doesn't come to fruition. Does that mean it's not resurrection? I wondered if I had understood my story all wrong. As I transitioned and more and more people faded from my life, as my friends reacted to me differently, as my mother grew more distant, as my wife and I moved toward divorce, I wondered if I had made the right decision. Maybe I could have toughed it out without transitioning, I pondered; after all, I had made it twenty-six years being perceived as female. Surely I could have made it longer.

I wondered if my transition was worth it when I realized what I would lose. Maybe I was being selfish. Maybe it was unfair for me to expect people to treat me differently. Maybe it was selfish to ask them to walk with me on my path. The negative, incomplete messages that I had received as a kid in church came back: What you want doesn't matter; it's only what God wants. Be humble. Be small. Let God do whatever God wants with you.

Was I making a mistake? Was I straying from the true path? It was a torturous thought cycle made worse by the fraying of my relationships.

But there were certain moments. Moments when I was alone. When I could finally catch my breath for a couple of minutes. Moments when I was able to still myself enough to silence all of the doubting voices in my head—the voices of my friends, the voice of my wife, the voice of my mother—all of those voices faded to silence and it was just me. And I was happy. Actually, deeper than that—I was at peace. Yes, things were hard and messy. Yes, the future was unknown. Yes, I might still be losing everything, but the feeling bloomed from my gut up into my heart and I exhaled peace. I sat and was actually present in my body. I could feel it in ways I had never felt it before. I wasn't trying to run from my skin; I was settled into it. I was in my body, and my body was me, and for the first time I felt full integration.

Resurrection isn't a moment; it's a process.

ᴖᴖ

The resurrection accounts of Jesus are varied. In the Gospel of Mark, thought to be the earliest of the Gospels, there is no evidence of the resurrection recorded beyond an angel's announcement in Mark 16:6-7 (the description of Jesus's post-resurrection encounter with Mary Magdalene in the garden and then appearance to his disciples in Mark 16:9-20 was added later). The earliest manuscript records have the story ending with all of Jesus's followers scattering, running away, and hiding. The movement was over. Done. They lost. Jesus was dead, his followers were afraid, and there was no hope left. They weren't waiting in hope of resurrection. They weren't waiting to be saved. They were waiting to be arrested and killed, so they hid.

Huddled in the upper room, they tried to piece together what had just happened. They were beyond planning for what was next and were simply lost in their terror. Everything Jesus had taught, everything he had promised, everything they thought they were a part of was gone.

These followers had left everything. They left their homes and their families; they left their jobs and their lives. They had been itinerant with Jesus for at least a few years. A lot of people thought they were deluded, foolish for believing in yet another messiah figure who would come to nothing. They must have been wondering if those naysayers were right after all. Was Jesus just like all of the other self-proclaimed messiahs? I don't blame the disciples for hiding.

In other gospel accounts we hear stories of resurrection, but even those stories are a little messy. In Matthew 28:1-9 and Luke 24:1-12, the women come to the tomb early in the morning in order to anoint Jesus's body for burial. They are the faithful ones, the ones who are determined to honor Jesus even in death. When they arrive, they find the tomb empty, and an angel asks why they are looking for the living among the dead. They run to tell the men and, unable to take the women's word for it, Peter and John run to the tomb to see for themselves.

In another account, Mary alone finds the tomb empty. She sees a man and thinks he's the gardener, and it's only after Jesus says her name that she believes it's him (John 20:11-18). Then, Jesus appears to the disciples in a locked room, but Thomas isn't with them, and so he doesn't believe. It is only when Jesus appears again a week later and allows Thomas to touch his scars that Thomas believes (John 20:20-29).

The stories are messy, not just because they are from different communities trying to make sense of what happened to turn terrified, hiding people into bold witnesses of Jesus's continued ministry, but also because it seems the appearances of a resurrected Jesus were a little messy. Jesus didn't walk out of the tomb perfected. In the story of Mary in the garden, her first response is to touch him, but he tells Mary not to cling to him because he's not ready yet (John 20:17). There was something still in process. His ability to appear in locked rooms, his appearing and disappearing—all of these point to a Jesus who was maybe a little less solid than he had been. A bit more ethereal. In the process of solidifying. Or maybe this was just how he was being perceived, as not quite the same. As someone who wasn't totally there anymore, but wasn't totally gone either. As someone who was in between worlds. Jesus was resurrected into a liminal space.

There were also Jesus's scars. Those scars in his hands and feet, that scar on his chest. His side wound. The scar on Jesus's chest captures my attention the most. Reverend Cameron Partridge first pointed out its significance to me in a workshop we did together at the Philadelphia Trans Health Conference in 2007. He talked about how in medieval paintings, Jesus's side wound was pictured as higher up, around his rib cage. It swooped a bit, near his chest.

"It's like the chest surgery scars of trans men." I was captivated. I fell in love with the painting of Thomas by Caravaggio. In that painting, Thomas and another disciple are gathered around checking out Jesus's scars. It does, indeed, look like a chest surgery scar. Later during that same conference, I would go to a chest surgery "show and tell" session. In a large conference room, transgender men stood in groups depending on who their surgeon had been. People who were considering chest surgery could then walk around and talk to people about their experience. Then, men around the room would take off their shirts so that you could see, in person, what their results were like.

It sounds kind of silly until you understand that this was one of the only ways members of the trans community could receive information. In the late 2000s, there were three chest surgery surgeons in the United States: one in California, one in Ohio, and one in Florida. Three surgeons in the whole of the United States. Three surgeons who required travel to receive care and cash payment up front, and, while they could do a phone consult, who often didn't communicate what you were going to experience until you'd already committed to the surgery.

These "show and tells" became holy ground for information sharing. Not just information, but also the sharing of bodies and skin. Scars and healing. We bared our bodies for one another because we knew that the medical establishment wasn't providing thorough information to us, and so we had to look out for each other. Some displayed their chest surgery results; others were witnesses to their transformation. We shared what it was like for us to be on testosterone, the long-term effects, all of it. We became our own longitudinal studies, our own medical journals. We had to. We told each other what we needed in order to recover, what surgery complications were like, what to look out for. We explained how we advocated for ourselves, what we said and did to get the attention that we needed. We kept detailed accounts in online diaries and shared them with others in our community.

We did it so that when you traveled to have surgery and you found yourself far from home in a hotel room post surgery, you didn't have to be so afraid. You knew what to look for. You knew that other people had been through this before. You knew there was healing on the other side.

At that 2007 conference, many of us were still waiting to schedule our surgery dates, waiting to be able to afford the travel and the hotel, and waiting to bank the time off of work. Waiting until we could find someone to travel with us and help us recover from surgery. For those of us waiting, these stories kept us going. They were the promise we had to look forward to. They were the vision of a future we were longing to inhabit.

Jesus's post-resurrection experiences feel so familiar to me. The longing to be seen as who I was becoming. The agony when I was still not visible. The liminal space of being not here but not yet there.

During seminary, I was hanging out in the lounge after a day of classes, chatting with people as they passed through, until it was time for me to catch my train back to New Jersey. A classmate came up to me casually, "Hey man." He paused. "You know, that's the first time I used male language for you without thinking about it." I smiled and said, "Good!" but inside there was still that twinge, still that piercing of the heart. There was the painful knowledge people were still thinking about my gender every time they related to me.

Would it ever get easier? Would I ever be able to put on a shirt without wondering how it made me look to other people? Would I ever be able to walk into a public restroom without feeling terror? Would my friends ever really see me as male? Would my family ever accept me?

These weren't superficial questions. They weren't about the clothing or my vanity. These were questions about safety. About access. About security. They were also questions about trust. Did people believe me when I told them who I was?

I think of Jesus and Thomas. The bearing of scars and the doubt. Would I always have to show people my scars? When I looked in the mirror, I didn't see how much I had changed. I saw only how far I still had to go.

Whatever our beliefs about a physical resurrection, we have to admit *something* must have happened to Jesus. Something happened that turned these terrified, scattering disciples who were hidden away behind locked doors in upper rooms into the bold, fierce people who would shout down crowds and proclaim the good news of Jesus in courts and under threats of beatings and prison. Something happened after Jesus died that made his followers get out of those locked rooms and into the streets. Something happened to them. Something convinced them that this movement, this story, this work wasn't over.

I'm struck by the intimacy in the post-resurrection stories. While there are one or two moments where Jesus is said to have appeared to large crowds (see 1 Cor. 15:6), most of the encounters are intimate. They are personal. They hint at reconciliation.

In the story of Mary mistaking Jesus for a gardener, Jesus simply says her name. Just one word is enough to cut through her panic and help her recognize her friend. I wonder if there was something about the way Jesus said Mary's name that was different from how other people said it. Did he have an accent? Pronounce it funny? Did he speak with a different kind of affection? Or was it her memory of when they met? When Jesus called through the fog in her mind to cast out the demons, and restored her to herself? In that previous moment of healing, did Mary hear her name through all of the other voices and know that this person calling her was someone she could trust? Then in the garden, at the height of her grief, did she again hear the voice she thought had been silenced forever? Mary is given the mission to tell the others. She becomes the first messenger of Jesus's resurrection. The vital resurrection story being entrusted to a woman—and not just any woman, a formerly possessed woman—disrupts the status quo. A woman whose word wouldn't have stood up in a court of law, a woman with no standing in society: she's given the message first. Once again, the way of Jesus is to subvert expectations and to offer hope to those on the margins of society.

Then there is the story of Jesus and Peter on the beach (John 21). After the horrific events of Jesus's death, after Peter had denied Jesus and run away, after hiding for fear of the religious authorities, Peter goes back to fishing. It's as if he's had his heart completely broken. The mission had fallen apart. They had all failed, so he returns to what he knows. No longer will he be a fisher of men. No longer will he be a part of the inner circle of the Messiah. Instead, he'll go home and try to get his life back. He'll rejoin the family business. He'll try to earn a decent wage. He'll pay his taxes and keep his head down. The radical and boisterous Peter has been cowed by the crucifixion. So Peter is out in a boat, fishing, when Jesus appears on the shore.

Instantly we see a spark of the old Peter: he puts his clothing back on, jumps into the water, and swims to shore. It's as if he needs the comfort of his clothes to shore up his courage. (How is this man going to lead the new movement if he can't even manage his own emotions?)

They sit down on the beach for breakfast and Jesus asks Peter three times if Peter loves him. Three opportunities to reverse three denials. Each question must have been a stinging wound. A reminder of Peter's failure, a reminder that Jesus knew how badly he failed. Peter needed to insist three times that he did love Jesus. He needed to be given the charge to do the work, to get back on mission; three times voiced to overcome the three betrayals. This exchange is a moment of pain, of intimate hurt, of reconciliation. Jesus is trying to help Peter move beyond his failings to do the work he's called to do. Peter, even as he's being given a second chance, is worried about the fate of the other guys in the circle and Jesus has to rebuke him again (see John 21:22). Maybe after that final rebuke it all sinks in for Peter. Maybe he finally understands what it is that he needs to do.

Post resurrection, Jesus also appears to two travelers on the road to Emmaus (Luke 24:13–32). Two people walking away from Jerusalem. Maybe two more people abandoning the movement, thinking that it's over. The person they thought could bring about change is dead and so its time to go home and get back to living. Maybe its time for them to get out of town so they won't be killed, too. As the stranger asks them questions, they are incredulous that anyone wouldn't know the events of what transpired in Jerusalem. How could something that so rocked their world remain unknown to others?

These quiet moments, these intimate revelations, are the hallmark of the resurrection. Jesus didn't storm into the places of power and prove himself. Jesus didn't rally the troops for another go. Some will point to this and say it's because the resurrection didn't actually happen; others will say it's because the political triumph will happen when Jesus comes back a second time. Another way to look at it might be resurrection being different than we expect it. Our humanity wants a redemption story. An underdog wins. We want those religious authorities to be scattered, we want the oppressed to rise up and take over the streets, we want the victory. These resurrection stories seem to indicate that reconciliation is found in person-to-person encounters. In the way a friend says your name, in the forgiveness offered even when you don't deserve it, in the recognition of your new reality. When we hold space for one another's resurrections and when we are seen in our own resurrections, we have courage to take up the work again. We have the courage to get back into the fight. We have the courage to believe that even death is not the final word.

We begin to look for others who have experienced what we've experienced. We find one person who will let us know we are not alone. One person to walk beside us. One person who understands, at least a little bit, what it's like to be us.

Many people in the transgender community are in isolation. They don't know anyone else who is trans. Their only connection with their own community is on the internet (which is better than it used to be, at least).[1] They watch television and movies and barely ever see anyone who looks like them.[2] Even as representation begins to change, it's still not enough. The stories about transgender people still too often focus on our bodies or tragedy. We need stories of transgender love. Stories of celebration. Stories of romance. We need stories not of death, but of resurrection.

The hope of resurrection isn't some "It gets better!" slogan slapped onto a product advertisement. It's not about everything finally being perfect after you die and get to heaven. The hope of resurrection is rooted in the here and now. A gritty, tenacious, scrappy hope that lets you know hanging on is worth it. It says that staying and fighting is important. We don't give up and go back to Emmaus or to our old lives as fishermen; we stay in Jerusalem and pick up the dropped torch. We don't scatter once the leader has been slain; we figure out how the work continues. We don't quit in the face of harassment. We look at our scars and call them beautiful.

This hope isn't expressed to gloss over the pain of crucifixion or glorify suffering. I no longer believe in redemptive suffering like I did when I was growing up. I don't believe that God tortures me to teach me. The church sign I once saw that said "Sometimes God has to break you to make you" makes me sick. That's an abusive God. But the idea of God's incarnation, God being with us in the muck and the mess? That's something I can get behind. God using the dirt to make something beautiful. God redeeming what people had intended for evil and turning it into something good, in spite of it all. The great mystery. The hope of salvation.

I thought someday my transition would be over, that there would be an end point. I would somehow "arrive." Now I know arrival never occurs, not really. There is always more to learn; there are always new ways to grow. There is always more to unlearn; there are always more ways to continue to root out the oppressor inside of me. I can continue to grapple with privilege, grapple with assumptions that don't match my lived reality, and yet still shape how I move through the world around me. This, too, is the process of resurrection.

Today, I wake up and get out of bed. I'm groggy; mornings have never agreed with me. I stumble to the bathroom to brush my teeth. I run my hand over the stubble on my face. I need to shave every day now if I want to be fully clean shaven. It still hasn't gotten old. After my shower I throw on a clean pair of boxers and some jeans and pull a t-shirt over my head. I don't think about what I'm wearing. I know when I go outside, I will be seen as who I am. I know that I will be visible. I also know the work isn't over, not in myself and not in my community.

This is the process of resurrection.

Conclusion

Just as coming out isn't a one-time thing and neither is transitioning, nor is our theological journey fixed. To quote J. R. R. Tolkien, "The road goes ever on."

The allure, for some, of American evangelicalism is its tidy systems and set beliefs. No need for questions or wrestling because everything is set out for you. No need to wonder if you've got it right because someone has told you what's right. No need to continue to grapple because truth never changes.

For some, the challenge of expansive traditions of Christianity is the lack of set of rules or answers or beliefs. There is an inherent need for questions, for wrestling, for grappling. There is a need for deep thinking. There is a need to keep working out your salvation with fear and trembling. It's hard work. It's continuous work. No wonder so many people want to write off progressive Christianity as "anything goes" so they can dismiss the deeper thought process behind it. There are similar parallels to gender expansiveness. We know this work is done best in community, with a core of justice behind it. Our ethics centers community and centers the well-being of the most marginalized. Following Jesus demands something of us beyond praying a prayer and going to heaven when we die. It requires us to work out our faith here and now, within the unjust systems of the world. It's hard. Some days I wish I *could* simply say a prayer and go about my day.

What I realized when I left evangelicalism and came out (more than once) is that I am responsible for my life and my faith. I can't allow them to be handled or dictated by some external authority. There is no one who can tell me exactly how to read the Bible or how to understand my gender or my body. This isn't to say I don't listen to advice or learn from others, because I do! I read deeply and broadly and seek out mentors for faith and life. I pay attention to tradition and interpretation. I learn from scholars and from the experiences of others. My life and faith are informed by my connections with other people who are living out their own faith. I am continually being taught and held accountable by the communities of which I am a part. I strive to learn from people who belong to other marginalized communities. This also means I cannot hand over authority and by doing so shrug off any of my own responsibility.

When I was more rigid in my beliefs, I could refuse to bake a cake for a gay couple, or picket an abortion clinic screaming invectives at young women. I could storm a building and terrify people and then, when asked about my tirade, simply say, "God made me do it. My pastor told me to." No personal responsibility required, no wrestling with whether the action was right or wrong, no internal questioning to consider, and always offloading the blame to someone else. These are the unfortunate hallmarks of certain pockets of evangelicalism.

Progressive Christianity asks participants to weigh every decision in light of our own consciences, our place in the world, our ethics, our understanding of God's values, and so much more. It can make every decision (from the purchase of a particular book to a decision about whether or not to have children in light of the global climate crisis) take on an incredible weight. Progressive Christians refuse to be satisfied by the simple claim, "My pastor told me this is what this verse means." Faith demands all of us—our intellect, our discipline, our hearts and souls. In many ways, it's harder to do right in progressive Christianity because we are aware of the many, many oppressive systems in which we are complicit. We realize we might be a part of sin without our knowledge, and our progressive understanding of faith means simply praying a prayer won't let us off the hook. Action is required.

Why stay in Christianity at all? It's a question I get asked all of the time, from people on all sides. Evangelicals wonder why I stay in a faith that I "clearly don't believe in" (perhaps simply because I don't believe like them). Queer and trans folks wonder why I stay in a church that has done so much harm to my community over the centuries. Depending on my relationship with the person asking and my mood, sometimes I'm witty: "I stay because I'm stubborn." Sometimes I answer: "I don't know why I stay, because it's exhausting."

In my heart of hearts, my answer is this: I stay because I find meaning in this Jesus story. There is something so captivating about Jesus, God taking on human flesh. Jesus who cares about and centers the marginalized, Jesus who heals the sick and makes really good wine, Jesus who hangs out with all of the freaks, Jesus who speaks truth to power. Jesus who is executed by both religious and political power. Jesus who defies even the authority of nature to be resurrected.

More than that, I also find meaning in the way these Jesus stories have been passed down. How people have struggled to make sense of them and to find themselves in the larger Christian story. How people have continually read the stories of Jesus in light of their own lived experiences and found a connection to the Divine and to one another. From liberation theology in Latin America to

Black theology, to feminist theology and womanist theology, to queer theology and now to trans theology. I am part of a lineage of people who are trying to find themselves in this story.

I stay because no one owns the story. No one gets to say that I don't belong in this church, in this tradition, in this faith. No one has the power to kick me out; what God has joined together, let no one separate. I stay because this tradition is mine, too.

Finally, I stay in Christianity because this story and the rituals of the church hold deep meaning for me. They have been the language I have been wrapped in since birth and they have given me language for my own journey. Even in all of my deconstruction and reconstruction the simple truth is this: this Jesus story gives me life.

This tradition can also be yours and give you life, too, if you want it. Wrestling with it, fighting with it, questioning yet sticking to it is worth the pain and the struggle. It's worth it to find new ways to think and believe. It's worth it to do the work to find your own meaning.

The road goes ever on. I'm grateful to walk it beside you.

Glossary

Black theology: A theological perspective that centers the lives and experiences of Black people, starting in the United States and later spreading to other parts of the world.

Clobber verses: The six Bible passages most often used to condemn LBG folks (Genesis 19; Leviticus 18:22 and 20:13; Romans 1:21-28; 1 Corinthians 6:9-10; 1 Timothy 1:10). A few additional verses used against transgender folks are these: Genesis 1; Deuteronomy 22:5; Deuteronomy 23:1.

Cisgender: Someone whose gender identity matches the sex they were assigned at birth.

Exvangelical: A term used by people who have left the evangelical church. Some have stayed in Christian faith; others have left it entirely. This term was coined by Blake Chastain as a way for people who grew up in similar environments to connect with one another.

Feminist theology: A theological perspective that centers the concerns and perspectives of women.

Gender expansiveness: An umbrella term for when people understand, embody, and express gender outside of the gender binary.

Gender expression: The way a person expresses their gender to the world. This could be through dress, mannerisms, or more.

Gender nonconforming: A person whose presentation of their gender falls outside of what is considered "typical."

Gender identity: A person's intrinsic understanding of their gender.

Liberation theology: A grouping of theologies written from the perspective of marginalized communities. Liberation theology came first out of the Latin American context but has now branched out into other contexts as well. Black theology, Queer theology, Feminist theology, and more all fall under the liberation theology umbrella.

Nonbinary: Someone who identifies outside of the male/female gender binary.

Polyamory: The act of having more than one intimate relationship at a time, with the consent of all involved.

Pronoun: A noun used to refer to people. People's pronouns can't always be guessed based on a person's appearance. The most common pronouns are he, she, and they, but many other pronouns exist (such as hir/hirs, ae/aer/aers, and fae/faer/faers).

Queer theology: A theological perspective that centers the experiences of queer people.

Sex assigned at birth: The label medical professionals use for babies when they are born, based on their genitalia. Trans folks use this to differentiate between the sex assigned to them by someone else and the gender they know themselves to be.

Sexual orientation: Words used to describe who you find yourself attracted to sexually.

Stealth: A term used by some transgender people to describe not being out as transgender after transitioning.

Transgender: A person whose gender identity differs from the sex they were assigned at birth.

Transgender theology: A theological perspective that centers the experiences of transgender and nonbinary people.

Womanist theology: A theological perspective that centers the experiences of Black women.

Further Reading

BIBLE AND THEOLOGY

Bawer, Bruce. *Stealing Jesus: How Fundamentalism Betrays Christianity*. New York: Crown Publishers, 1997. Bawer traces the rise of evangelicalism in the United States while also looking at many of the beliefs considered "unchanging" and uncovering their origins. A formative book from my own journey out of fundamentalistic evangelicalism.

Borg, Marcus. *Reading the Bible Again for the First Time: Taking the Bible Seriously but Not Literally*. San Francisco: HarperSanFrancisco, 2001. Borg takes readers who grew up with a literalist interpretation of the Bible on a journey to understand different ways to read the Scriptures.

Keck, Leander E., ed. *New Interpreter's Bible Commentary*. 10 vols. Nashville: Abingdon, 1994-2004. These are hefty books, but they provide accessible deep dives into both the history and the interpretation of texts.

Scanzoni, Letha Dawson, and Virginia Ramey Mollenkott. *Is the Homosexual My Neighbor? A Positive Christian Response*. Revised edition. San Francisco: HarperSanFranciso, 1994. Mollenkott and Scanzoni offer strong arguments about the biblical texts often used to argue against LGBTQ+ people.

Further Reading

TRANSGENDER IDENTITY

Hartke, Austen. *Transforming: The Bible and the Lives of Transgender Christians*. Louisville: Westminster John Knox, 2018. Hartke shares some of his story of coming out and transitioning as well as delving into what the Bible says (and doesn't say) about gender expansive people. Hartke also shares the stories of other trans Christians and how they've grappled with faith and gender identity.

Kailey, Matt. *Just Add Hormones: An Insider's Guide to the Transsexual Experience*. Boston: Beacon, 2004. Part memoir and part informational guide, this conversational book explains gender identity and the process of medical transition.

McBee, Thomas Page. *Amateur: A Reckoning with Gender, Masculinity, and Identity*. Edinburgh: Canongate, 2018. A memoir on grappling with masculinity as a transgender man. Heart wrenching and beautiful.

Paige, Chris. *OtherWise Christian: A Guidebook for Transgender Liberation*. Eugene: OtherWise Engaged Publishing, 2019. In this book Mx. Paige pulls together many different streams of thinking and writing about trans people and theology.

Sabia-Tanis, Justin. *Trans-Gender: Theology, Ministry, and Communities of Faith*. 2nd ed. Eugene: Wipf & Stock, 2017. A phenomenal introductory book that not only tackles the frequently asked questions about the trans experience but also examines the Bible verses usually used to condemn transgender individuals. Sabia-Tanis then delves into how the church can be more welcoming.

QUEER THEOLOGY

Cheng, Patrick. *Radical Love: An Introduction to Queer Theology*. New York: Seabury Books, 2011. In this introduction to queer theology, Cheng walks readers through various streams of thinking about LGBTQ+ issues and theology. An accessible book with discussion questions to dive deeper.

The Queer Bible Commentary, edited by Deryn Guest, Robert E. Goss, Mona West, and Thomas Bohache. London: SCM, 2015. This commentary offers queer and trans readings of many different portions of Scripture. Instead of using a verse-by-verse approach, the authors look at stories and themes to see where queerness can be found.

QueerTheology.com. A website that is both accessible and theologically serious. It aims to further the conversation about LGBTQ+ issues and the church.

Notes

CHAPTER 1

1. See the discussion of eunuchs in chapter 16 of Chris Paige, *OtherWise Christian: A Guidebook for Transgender Liberation* (Eugene: OtherWise Engaged Publishing, 2019).

2. See also the discussion of Deuteronomy in *New Interpreter's Bible Commentary*, ed. Leander E. Keck, 10 vols. (Nashville: Abingdon, 1994–2004), vol. 1.

3. For more, see chapter 16 of Paige, *OtherWise Christian*.

4. Both statistics are from Jeffrey M. Jones, "LGBT Identification Rises to 5.6% in Latest U.S. Estimate," Gallup Report (February 24, 2021), https://news.gallup.com/poll/329708/lgbt-identification-rises-latest-estimate.aspx.

5. "Cleveland Clinic Survey: Men Will Do Almost Anything to Avoid Going to the Doctor," Cleveland Clinic Newsroom (September 4, 2019), https://newsroom.clevelandclinic.org/.2019/09/04/cleveland-clinic-survey-men-will-do-almost-anything-to-avoid-going-to-the-doctor/; Laurel Kiesel, "Women and Pain: Disparities in Experience and Treatment," Harvard Health Blog (October 9, 2017), https://www.health.harvard.edu/blog/women-and-pain-disparities-in-experience-and-treatment-2017100912562; "National Transgender Discrimination Sur-

vey: Full Report," National Center for Transgender Equality (September 11, 2012), https://transequality.org/issues/resources/national-transgender-dis crimination-survey-full-report.

6. "Study: Transgender Teens' Suicide Risk Higher Than Cisgender Peers'," Pittwire (January 21, 2020), https://www.pitt.edu/pittwire/fea tures-articles/study-transgender-teens-suicide-risk-higher-cisgender -peers; Greta R. Bauer et al., "Intervenable Factors Associated with Suicide Risk in Transgender Persons: A Respondent driven Sampling Study in Ontario, Canada," BMC Public Health (June 2, 2015), https://bmcpub lichealth.biomedcentral.com/articles/10.1186/s12889-015-1867-2.

CHAPTER 2

1. See also chapter 1 of *The Queer Bible Commentary*, ed. Deryn Guest et al. (London: SCM, 2015), for more about Jacob.

2. While many conservative evangelicals treat Abraham's willingness to sacrifice Isaac as a sign of obedience, Jewish tradition questions that interpretation. See chapter 2 of *The Soul of the Stranger: Reading God and Torah from a Transgender Perspective* by Joy Ladin (Waltham, MA: Brandeis University Press, 2019), for discussion of the trauma this would have caused Isaac. On this story being about Abraham's failure, see Rabbi Hyim Shafner, "Did Abraham Fail His Final Test?," https://morethodoxjudaism.wordpress .com/2010/10/12/did-abraham-fail-his-final-test-by-rabbi-hyim-shafner/.

3. For more on interpretations of this garment see chapter 19 of Paige, *OtherWise Christian*.

CHAPTER 3

1. For more see Richard Plant, *The Pink Triangle: The Nazi War against Homosexuals* (New York: Holt, 1986), and Heinz Heger, *The Men with the Pink Triangle: The True, Life-or-Death Story of Homosexuals in the Nazi Death Camps*, trans. David Fernbach, rev. ed. (Boston: Alyson Publications, 1994).

CHAPTER 4

1. Jaime M. Grant et al., "Injustice at Every Turn: A Report of the Transgender Discrimination Survey," https://transequality.org/sites/default/files/docs/resources/NTDS_Report.pdf.

2. Jody L. Herman et al., "Suicide Thoughts and Attempts among Transgender Adults: Findings from the 2015 U.S. Transgender Survey," UCLS School of Law Williams Institute, https://williamsinstitute.law.ucla.edu/publications/suicidality-transgender-adults/.

CHAPTER 9

1. Jaime M. Grant et al., "Injustice at Every Turn: A Report of the Transgender Discrimination Survey," https://transequality.org/sites/default/files/docs/resources/NTDS_Report.pdf.

2. Quotations from the Gospel of Thomas are from Thomas O. Lambdin's translation, found at https://www.marquette.edu/maqom/Gospel%20of%20Thomas%20Lambdin.pdf.

CHAPTER 10

1. See Julie Woulfe and Melina Wald, "The Impact of the COVID-19 Pandemic on the Transgender and Non-Binary Community," https://www.columbiapsychiatry.org/news/impact-covid-19-pandemic-transgender-and-non-binary-community.

2. See the "Where We Are on TV Report—2020," GLAAD Media Institute, https://www.glaad.org/wherewereontv20.